Communications
in Computer and Information Science 495

Jian Cao   Lijie Wen   Xiao Liu (Eds.)

Process-Aware Systems

First International Workshop, PAS 2014
Shanghai, China, October 17, 2014
Proceedings

 Springer

Volume Editors

Jian Cao
Shanghai Jiaotong University, China
E-mail: cao-jian@sjtu.edu.cn

Lijie Wen
Tsinghua University, Beijing, China
E-mail: wenlj@tsinghua.edu.cn

Xiao Liu
East China Normal University
Shanghai, China
E-mail: xliu@sei.ecnu.edu.cn

ISSN 1865-0929   e-ISSN 1865-0937
ISBN 978-3-662-46169-3   e-ISBN 978-3-662-46170-9
DOI 10.1007/978-3-662-46170-9
Springer Heidelberg New York Dordrecht London

Library of Congress Control Number: 2015931556

Typesetting: Camera-ready by author, data conversion by Scientific Publishing Services, Chennai, India

Printed on acid-free paper

Springer is part of Springer Science+Business Media (www.springer.com)

Preface

This volume collects the proceedings of the First International Workshop on Process-Aware Systems (PAS 2014) held in Shanghai, China, on October 17, 2014, co-located with the 4th Chinese Conference on Business Process Management (China BPM 2014). PAS 2014 is a cross-area international workshop on process-aware systems. It aims at bringing together researchers, developers, users, and practitioners interested in process management, and formally exploring various potentials about process management and process thinking in the era of cloud computing and big data from the perspective of both academia and industry. The short-term development goal of PAS is to become an international conference in the next two years.

As the first edition in this workshop/conference series, PAS 2014 attracted only a relatively small number of submissions: 14 (qualified) submissions. These submissions reported on up-to-date research findings of scholars from three countries (China, Colombia, and Korea). After each submission was reviewed by at least three Program Committee members, five full papers and three short papers were accepted for publication in this volume of conference proceedings (i.e., 35.7% acceptance rate for full papers and 21.4% for short papers). These eight papers cover various topics that can be categorized under four main research focuses in BPM, including process modeling and comparison (two papers), workflow scheduling and resource allocation (three papers), scientific workflow verification (one paper), and workflow applications (two papers).

We would like to thank the Program Committee members for their thorough reviews and discussions of the submitted papers. We express our gratitude to other conference committees as well, especially to the general chairs, Jianmin Wang and Yun Yang, and the Steering Committee for their valuable guidance, to the organization chair, Feng Li, and other staff at Donghua University for their attentive preparations for this workshop, to the publication chair, Xiao Liu, for his efforts in the preparation and publication of the workshop proceedings, and to the publicity chairs, Hongyan Zhang and Jihong Liu, for their efforts in publishing workshop updates and promoting the workshop in the region. Last but not least, we are thankful to the authors of the submissions, the presenters, and all the other workshop participants, because the workshop could not be held without their contributions and interest.

October 2014

Jian Cao
Lijie Wen

Organization

PAS 2014 was organized in Shanghai, China, by Donghua University.

Steering Committee

Jianmin Wang	Tsinghua University, China
Chongyi Yuan	Peking University, China
Liang Zhang	Fudan University, China
Jianwen Su	The University of California, Santa Barbara, USA
Arthur ter Hofstede	Queensland University of Technology, Australia

General Chairs

Jianmin Wang	Tsinghua University, China
Yun Yang	Swinburne University of Technology, Australia

Program Chairs

Jian Cao	Shanghai Jiao Tong University, China
Lijie Wen	Tsinghua University, China

Organization Chair

Feng Li	Donghua University, China

Publicity Chairs

Hongyan Zhang	Beijing Jiaotong University, China
Jihong Liu	Beihang University, China

Publication Chair

Xiao Liu	East China Normal University, China

Program Committee

Marco Aiello	University of Groningen, The Netherlands
Luciano Garcia Banuelos	University of Tartu, Estonia
Kamel Barkaoui	Cedric CNAM Paris, France
Jian Cao	Shanghai Jiao Tong University, China
Mingsong Chen	East China Normal University
Lizhen Cui	Shangdong University, China
Florian Daniel	University of Trento, Italy
Wanchun Dou	Nanjing University, China
Rik Eshuis	Eindhoven University of Technology, The Netherlands
Zaiwen Feng	Wuhan University, China
Tao Hu	Hainan University, China
Akhil Kumar	Penn State University, USA
Jianxun Liu	Hunan University of Science and Technology, China
Min Liu	Tongji University, China
Rong Liu	IBM Research, USA
Xiao Liu	East China Normal University, China
Zongwei Luo	Hong Kong University, Hong Kong
Shiyong Lv	Wayne State University, USA
Fabrizio Maria Maggi	University of Tartu, Estonia
Massimo Mecella	Sapienza University of Rome, Italy
Chun Ouyang	Queensland University Of Technology, Australia
Kaijun Ren	National University of Defense Technology, China
Zhe Shan	University of Cincinnati, USA
Minseok Song	Ulsan National Institute of Science and Technology, Korea
Jianwen Su	The University of California, Santa Barbara, USA
Josep Carmona Vargas	Polytechnic University of Catalonia, Spanish
Li Wan	Huazhong University of Science and Technology, China
Jiacun Wang	Monmouse University, USA
Jianmin Wang	Tsinghua University, China
Mingzhong Wang	Beijing Institute of Technology, China
Zhongjie Wang	Harbin Institute of Technology, China
Barbara Weber	University of Innsbruck, Austria
Jun Wei	Institute of Software, CAS, China
Matthias Weidlich	Imperial College London, UK
Lijie Wen	Tsinghua University, China
Raymond Wong	University of New South Wales, Australia

Jinhua Xiong   Institute of Computing Technology, CAS,
                                   China
Dong Yang   Donghua University, China
Jian Yang   Macquarie University, Australia
Yun Yang   Swinburne University of Technology, Australia
Jianwei Yin   Zhejiang University, China
Yang Yu   Sun Yat-Sen University, China
Chongyi Yuan   Peking University, China
Liang Zhang   Fudan University, China
Yang Zhang   Beijing University of Posts and
                                   Telecommunications, China

Table of Contents

Process Modeling and Comparison

Petri Net Based Behavior Description of Cross-Organization Workflow
with Synchronous Interaction Pattern 1
  Cong Liu, Qingtian Zeng, Hua Duan, and Faming Lu

A New Similarity Search Approach on Process Models 11
  Siyun Li and Jian Cao

Workflow Scheduling and Resource Allocation

Workflow Scheduling in Grid Based on Bacterial Foraging
Optimization 21
  *Feng Yao, Jidong Ge, Chuanyi Li, Yuhang Ge, Haiyang Hu,
  Yu Zhou, Hao Hu, and Bin Luo*

Research on Workflow Scheduling Algorithms in the Cloud 35
  Congyang Chen, Jianxun Liu, Yiping Wen, and Jinjun Chen

Q-learning Algorithm for Task Allocation Based on Social Relation 49
  Xingmei Liu, Jian Chen, Yu Ji, and Yang Yu

Scientific Workflow Verification

Temporal Verification for Scientific Cloud Workflows: State-of-the-Art
and Research Challenges 59
  Qiudan Wang, Xiao Liu, Zhou Zhao, and Futian Wang

Workflow Applications

Quality Control Method in Crowdsourcing Platform for Professional
Dictionary Compilation Process (PDCCP) 75
  Shanshan Feng, Xiao Li, and Huisi Ou

HelpMe: A Heuristic License Plate Correction Method for Big Data
Application 93
  Guochao Jia, Xu Tao, Yan Liu, and Wanchun Dou

Author Index 109

Petri Net Based Behavior Description of Cross-Organization Workflow with Synchronous Interaction Pattern

Cong Liu[1,2], Qingtian Zeng[2,3], Hua Duan[4], and Faming Lu[1,2]

[1] The Key Laboratory of Embedded System and Service Computing,
Ministry of Education, Tongji University, Shanghai 200092, China
[2] College of Information Science and Engineering,
Shandong University of Science and Technology, Qingdao 266590, China
[3] College of Electronic Communication,
Shandong University of Science and Technology, Qingdao 266590, China
[4] College of Mathematics, Shandong University of Science and Technology,
Qingdao 266590, China
{liucongchina,qtzeng,huaduan59,fm_lu}@163.com

Abstract. Today's workflow systems are crossing organizational boundaries and usually involve multiple organizations or partners, and the cross-organization workflow has received much public attention from both the academia and the industry. This way the property analysis as well as system control for a cross-organization workflow is very important. In this paper, we focus on a kind of loosely coupled workflow architecture with synchronous interaction pattern, i.e. each organization owns its private workflow process and can operate independently, and they need to synchronize through certain tasks. Its behavior description approach is obtained using the synchronized shuffle operation of Petri net language. It is proved that our approach benefits the behavior characterization of cross-organizational workflow with synchronous interaction pattern and can be further used to decide and control the fairness, liveness, deadlock and trap for the cross-organization workflow. A running case of cross-organizational medical diagnosis workflow is given to validate our approaches throughout the whole paper.

Keywords: Cross-organization workflow, Synchronous Interaction Pattern, Behavior Description, Petri Net Language.

1 Introduction

With the ever-accelerated development of modern information system, more and more business processes are crossing organizational boundaries and calling for multiple organizations to corporate [1]. This way the cross-organization workflow has received much public attention from both the academia and the industry. To support the cross-organizational workflows, several conceptual architectures, including capacity sharing, chained execution, subcontracting, case transfer, extended case transfer and loosely coupled, are surveyed by Aalst [2]. This work focuses on a kind of loosely coupled

J. Cao et al. (Eds.): PAS 2014, CCIS 495, pp. 1–10, 2015.

workflow architecture [3], i.e. each individual organization owns its private business workflow and can operate independently. To accomplish certain business missions, these loosely-coupled organizations need to corporate or interact with each other at certain points. In this way, synchronization or interaction between different organizations commonly exists. Generally speaking, there are two kinds of interaction mechanisms: asynchronous interaction patterns and synchronous interaction patterns. The asynchronous interaction patterns consisting of the message interaction pattern and resource interaction pattern while the synchronous interaction pattern specific refers to task synchronization pattern, i.e. different organizations collaborate in some specific tasks at the same time. For more detailed explanations on these four different interaction patterns, please see [4]-[5]. To analyze and control the whole cross-organizational workflow is an extremely difficult task as different organizations and interaction patterns are involved. Fortunately, the behavior description of a cross-organization workflow provides an effective solution for its analysis and control. In this paper, we mainly address the methodology to character the behavior of cross-organization workflow with synchronous interaction pattern.

As Petri nets are a type of well-founded process modeling technique and they have been widely used to model, analyze, control and verify workflows [6]-[9], we lay our research on the basis of Petri net theory [10]-[12]. There are at least three main reasons for using them to model and analyze workflows [9]: (1) Graphical nature and formal semantics; (2) the explicit model of a case state; and (3) the availability of many analysis techniques. As Petri net language is a set sequence of firings of transitions for describing the Petri net behavior. Therefore, we investigate the behavior description of cross-organizational workflow model using Petri net language theory. More specifically, we investigate the behavior descriptions of cross-organizational workflow with task synchronization pattern using the synchronized shuffle operation of Petri net language.

The remainder of this paper is organized as follows. Section 2 discusses the related work. Section 3 introduces basic concept of Petri net and WF-net. In Section 4, CWF-net is proposed to model the cross-organization workflow model with task synchronization pattern. Section 5 introduces behavior descriptions of CWF-net based on the synchronized shuffle operation of Petri net language. Finally, Section 6 draws concluding remarks.

2   Related Work

Aalst considered that workflows distributed over a number of organizations. Two important questions were well addressed in his work [1]-[3]: (1) the minimal requirements of inter- organizational workflow, and (2) how to decide whether an inter-organizational workflow, modeled with Petri nets, is consistent with an interaction structure specified through a message sequence. In [16], Schulz and Orlowska focused on three aspects to support the execution of cross-organizational workflows that have been modeled with a process view approach: (1) communication between the entities, (2) their impact on an extended workflow engine, and (3) the design of cross-organizational workflow architecture. A Petri-Net-based state transition approach that binds states of private workflow tasks to their adjacent workflow view-task was introduced. The concepts are demonstrated by a scenario, run by two extended workflow management systems. Jiang et al. [17] described a timed colored Petri net and process-view combined approach to construct cross-organizational workflows, and a three-model framework was proposed to realize the interoperability of cross-organizational workflows. Finally, a case study of the collaborative development of a motorcycle was presented to verify the validity of our approach. In our previous work, we formally defined different cross-organizational coordination patterns, including message interaction pattern, resource interaction pattern, task collaboration pattern, service outsourcing pattern, and etc. based on RM_WF_Net in our precisely work [4], whose correctness is verified by constructing its corresponding reachability graph. To analyze the property of workflow net systems, the language description is also an important approach. With the formal language expression, we can decide and control the fairness, liveness, deadlock and trap for the workflow processes, which provides an effective solution for the property analysis based on Petri net. Following this approach, Yan et al. proposed a net reduction rules to preserve languages of workflow net systems, and based on which a generation algorithm is proposed for the language expression of workflow net systems in [18]. This method contributes to solve the explosion problem for reachable state space to a certain degree.

Based on the above-mentioned literature review, we can conclude that most of previous research on the modeling and analysis of cross-organization workflow net focus on the modeling and structural analysis, and there is little work on the behavior description of cross-organization workflow net system. In this paper, we address the behavior description for a kind cross-organizational workflow with task synchronization pattern using Petri net language. As the first complete framework to perform the behavior description of cross-organizational workflow, we are sure that our work can improve the state-of-art to a great extent.

3   Preliminaries

Modeling approaches for workflows have been studied for decades, and some excellent models such as, WF-net, XPDL, BPEL, BPMN and etc., have been widely used. Whatever models are used, the workflow process is totally determined by tasks and their dependency relations. This work is based on Petri net and its language theory, WF-net to be more specific. We assume that readers are familiar with the basic concepts of Petri nets [10]-[12] and WF-net [9]. Some of the essential terminologies and notations are listed as follows.

Definition 3.1. A *Petri net* is a 4-tuple $\Sigma=(P, T; F, M_0)$, where: (1) $P=\{p_1, p_2, \ldots p_m\}$ is a finite set of places; (2) $T=\{t_1, t_2, \ldots t_n\}$ is a finite set of transitions; (3) $F\subseteq(P{\times}T)\cup(T{\times}P)$ is a finite set of arcs (flow relation); (4) $M_0: P\rightarrow\{0,1,2,3,\ldots\}$ is the initial marking; and (5) $P\cap T=\varnothing$ and $P\cup T\neq\varnothing$.

For all $x \in P \cup T$, the set ${}^\bullet x = \{y| \ y \in P \cup T \wedge (y, x) \in F\}$ is the pre-set of x, and $x^\bullet = \{y|$ $y \in P \cup T \wedge (x, y) \in F\}$ is the post-set of x. p is marked by M iff $M(p) > 0$. A transition $t \in T$ is enabled under M, if and only if $\forall p \in {}^\bullet t: M(p) > 0$, denoted as $M[t>$. If $M[t>$ holds, t may fire, resulting in a new marking M', denoted as $M[t>M'$, such that $M'(p) = M(p) - 1$ if $\forall p \in {}^\bullet t \setminus t^\bullet$, $M'(p) = M(p) + 1$ if $\forall p \in t^\bullet \setminus {}^\bullet t$, and otherwise $M'(p) = M(p)$. An initial marking is denoted by M_0 and $R(M_0)$ is defined as the set of all reachable marking set of Σ where $\forall M_i \in R(M_0)$ such that $M_0[\delta > M_i$.

Definition 3.2. Let $\Sigma = (P, T; F, M_0)$ be a Petri net. A place $p \in P$ is *bounded* if there is an non-negative integer n, such that $M_i(p) \leq n$ for all reachable markings $M_i \in R(M_0)$. A Petri net is *bounded* if all its places are bounded.

Boundedness is a decidable property which needs the construction of the coverability (or reachability) graph. If a place is found to be unbounded, a special symbol ω is introduced to indicate this fact.

A Petri net which models a workflow process definition is called the workflow net or WF-net whose definition is briefly reviewed following [9].

Definition 3.3. A *Petri net* $\Sigma = (P, T; F, M_0)$ is a WF-net if: (1) there is one source place $i \in P$ such that ${}^\bullet i = \varnothing$; (2) there is one sink place $o \in P$ such that $o^\bullet = \varnothing$; (3) Each node $x \in P \cup T$ is on a path from i to o; and (4) $\forall p \in P$, $M_0(p) = 1$ if $p = i$, and otherwise $M_0(p) = 0$.

As any process handled by the WF-net is created if it enters the workflow engine and is deleted when it is completed, it has an input place and an output place to represent these two states respectively. In a WF-net, the transition set T is used to represent the tasks in the workflow, and source place and sink place represent its start and end respectively. For the rest of this paper, a WF-net is formally denoted as $W = (P, T; F, M_0)$ to be distinguished from traditional Petri net. Moreover, as our WF-net is specifically used to model workflow processes, we synonymously use the term transition and task for convenience.

4   Petri Net Model for Cross-Organization Workflow with Synchronous Interaction Pattern

4.1   CWF-Net with Synchronous Interaction Pattern

When charactering the cross-organizational features of a loosely-coupled workflow, we often use different kinds of interaction patterns which contain asynchronous and synchronous ones [4]-[5]. The asynchronous interaction patterns involve the message interaction pattern and resource interaction pattern while the synchronous interaction pattern specific refers to task synchronization pattern. In this section, we only focus on a kind of cross-organization workflow with task synchronization pattern.

If two different organizations need to synchronize to finish a certain task, i.e., each organization shoulders parts of this task, in this way, there exists a task synchronization pattern between these two organizations. The formal definition of task synchronization pattern and the cross-organization workflow net with task synchronization pattern are defined in Definitions 4.1-4.2.

Definition 4.1. Let $W_1=(P_1, T_1; F_1, M_{01})$ and $W_2=(P_2, T_2; F_2, M_{02})$ be the WF-net of two workflow processes. A *task synchronization pattern* exist between them if (1) $P_1 \cap P_2 = \varnothing$; and (2) $T_1 \cap T_2 \neq \varnothing$.

Definition 4.2. Let $W_1=(P_1, T_1; F_1, M_{01})$ and $W_2=(P_2, T_2; F_2, M_{02})$ be the WF-net of two workflow processes. $W_{CW}=(P, T; F, M_0)$ is the cross-organization workflow net with task synchronization pattern, short for CWF-net, if: (1) $P=P_1 \cup P_2$; (2) $T=T_1 \cup T_2$; (3) $F=F_1 \cup F_2$; and (4) $M_0=M_{01} \cup M_{02}$.

4.2   A Typical Cross-Organization Workflow Case

A typical scenario of cross-organization medical diagnosis workflow process at least involves the surgical organization and the cardiovascular organization. For more information please refer to the case study in [6]. Part of this scenario is described as: (1) When a patient arrives, the outpatient medical staff performs pre-examination triage; (2) Then the patient information is generated based on the pre-examination result and sent to the surgical medical staff; (3) The surgical medical staff takes admissions and presents the reservation application, and then generates the reservation form; (4) The surgeon diagnoses this patient and determine if he needs a consultation with the cardiovascular internists; (5) If a consultation is needed, then the surgeon applies consultation by sending consultation form to the cardiovascular internists; (6) If there is no need to perform a consultation, the surgeon will give prescription based on the patient symptom; (7) The internists receive the consultation request and begin to arrange the consultation; (8) Surgeons and internists conduct the consultation and finally to give a prescription together; (9) The internists make the consultation summary; and (10) The patient takes the medicine and then leaves.

This cross-organization medical diagnosis workflow process involves two organizations, i.e., the surgical organization and the cardiovascular organization. More specifically, the surgical organization contains tasks, such as pre-examination triage (t_1), admissions (t_2), reservation application (t_3), diagnosis (t_4), consultation application (t_5), give prescription (t_6) and etc. The cardiovascular organization mainly consists of tasks like receive consultation request (t_7), consultation arrangement (t_8), consultation summary (t_{11}) and file archive (t_{12}). These two organizations need to collaborate to finish certain tasks, including consultation (t_9) and give prescription (t_{10}). Thus, there exists a task synchronization pattern between them.

According to the former business description, we obtain the WF-net s of the surgical organization (W_s) and the cardiovascular organization (W_C) which is shown in Figs. 1-2.

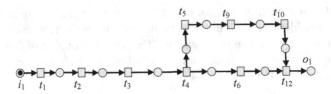

Fig. 1. WF-net of Surgical Organization (W_S)

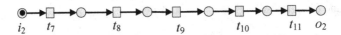

Fig. 2. WF-net of Cardiovascular Organization (W_C)

According to Definitions 4.1-4.2, we obtain the cross-organization workflow net, W_{CW}, of this medical diagnosis scenario as shown in Fig. 3.

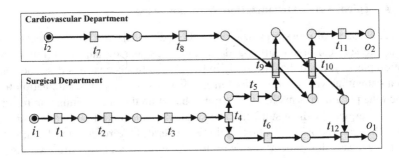

Fig. 3. CWF-net of the Medical Diagnosis Workflow (W_{CW})

5   Behavior Description of Cross-Organization Workflow with Synchronous Interaction Pattern

In this section, we analyze the behavior description of cross-organization workflow with synchronous interaction pattern. Our method is laid on the synchronized shuffle of Petri net languages, which is first introduced by Latteux [13]. Before rendering our approach, we will first review some of the basics on Petri net language and some limitations of our work.

In this paper, we focus on a kind of bounded Petri net, whose language is proved to be regular languages [11], thereby some commonly used language operators are reviewed as: *connection operator* "•", *choice operator* "+", *Kleen-closure operator* "*", and *parallel operator* "//". Please refer to [10]-[11] for more detailed introduction.

According to the theory of Petri net languages [12], four different types of languages named L-type, G-type, T-type and P-type are defined based on the difference of their terminal markings. Depending on the choice of transition labeling (free, λ-free, arbitrary), each type is divided into three classes. In this paper, we use the free

L-type language as example in the following discussion and the finite final marking set is defined as the subset of its reachable marking set $R(M_0)$.

$Q_T \subseteq R(M_0) \wedge (\forall M_e \in Q_T, \forall p \in P - P_f: M_e(p) = 0)$, where M_0 is the initial marking, P is the place set of a given Petri net $\Sigma = (P, T; F, M_0)$, and $P_f \in P$ is an appointed place set. The formal definition of Petri net language is presented in Definition 5.1. Let T^* stands for all possible strings of transition T including the empty one.

Definition 5.1[12]. Let $\Sigma = (P, T; F, M_0)$ be a Petri net, and $P_f \in P$. $L(\Sigma)$ is the language of Σ if $L(\Sigma) = \{ \delta | \delta \in T^* \wedge M_0[\delta > M_e \wedge (\forall p \in P - P_f: M_e(p) = 0)] \}$. P_f is named as the end place set of Σ.

During the following discussions about Petri net language, a Petri net is denoted directly as $\Sigma = (P, T; F, M_0, P_f)$ where P_f is the end place set. The end place set can be decided by users with different purposes based on the physical system.

The operation of synchronized shuffle of Petri net language is defined and applied in [13]-[14]. To present the definition of synchronized shuffle operation, several notations are introduced first.

Definition 5.2[13]. Let X be an alphabet. For any $a \in X$, we denote $\#(a, w)$ as the number of a occurring in the word w.

Definition 5.3[13]. Let X be an alphabet. For any language $L \subseteq X^*$, we denote the alphabet of L by $\delta(L) = \{ x \in X | \exists w \in L: \#(x, w) > 0 \}$.

For example, $\delta(a + b) = \delta(aa + aab) = \{ a, b \}$.

Definition 5.4[13]. Let X be an alphabet. We define the projection of X over the sub-alphabet Y such that $Y \subseteq X$, for each $x \in X$, if $x \in Y$ then $\Pi_{X \to Y}(x) = x$, otherwise $\Pi_{X \to Y}(x) = \varepsilon$.

The definition of synchronized shuffle of two Petri net languages is defined in Definition 5.5.

Definition 5.5[13]. Let X be an alphabet and $L(\Sigma_1)$, $L(\Sigma_2) \subseteq X^*$ be two different languages on X. The synchronized shuffle of $L(\Sigma_1)$ and $L(\Sigma_2)$, denoted as $L(\Sigma_1) \Theta L(\Sigma_2)$, is defined as: $L(\Sigma_1) \Theta L(\Sigma_2) = \{ w \in X^* | X = \delta(L(\Sigma_1)) \cup \delta(L(\Sigma_2)), \Pi_{X \to \delta(L(\Sigma_i))}(w) \in L(\Sigma_i), i \in \{1, 2\} \}$.

Similarly, the sharing synthesis of $L(\Sigma_i)$ ($i \in \{1, 2, 3...k\}$) denoted by $\overset{k}{\underset{i=1}{\Theta}} L(\Sigma_i)$, is defined as: $\overset{k}{\underset{i=1}{\Theta}} L(\Sigma_i) = ((L(\Sigma_1) \Theta L(\Sigma_2)) \Theta L(\Sigma_3)) \cdots \Theta L(\Sigma_k) = \overset{k-1}{\underset{i=1}{\Theta}} L(\Sigma_i) \Theta L(\Sigma_k)$.

According to Definition 5.5, it is easy to obtain that: (1) $bab \Theta cac = \{ bcabc, bcacb, cbabc, cbacb \}$, (2) $abc \Theta cba = \varnothing$, and (3) $ab \Theta a = \{ ab \}$.

Theorem 5.1. Let $W_i=(P_i, T_i; F_i, M_{0i}, P_{fi})$ $(i\in\{1, 2, 3...k\})$ be the WF-net of a workflow process and $W_{CW}=(P, T; F, M_0, P_f)$ is their corresponding cross-organization workflow net with task synchronization pattern. We have $L(W_{CW})=\Theta_{1\leq i\leq k}L(W_i)$.

Proof. Let $M_f\subseteq R(M_0)$, and $\forall M\in M_f$ such that $\forall p\in P-P_f$, $M(p)=0$, $M_{fi}=\{\Gamma_{P\to Pi}|M\in M_f\}$, $L(W_{CW})=\{\delta|\delta\in T^*\wedge M_0[\delta>M\wedge(M\in M_f)\}$.

Next, we prove this theorem by induction on $|\delta|$.

(1) If $|\delta|=1$, $\delta_i=\Pi_{T\to Ti}(\delta)=\delta$ if $\delta\in T_i$ and $\delta_i=\Pi_{T\to Ti}(\delta)=\epsilon$ otherwise, $(i\in\{1,2,3...k\})$.

With $\delta\in L(W_{CW})$ iff $M_0[\delta>M_1\wedge M_1\in M_f$, and iff $(\Gamma_{P\to Pi}(M_0)[\delta_i>\Gamma_{P\to Pi}(M_1))\wedge(\Gamma_{P\to Pi}(M_1)\in M_{fi})$, $\delta_i\in L(W_i)$ $(i\in\{1, 2, 3...k\})$.

(2) Suppose the conclusion is correct when$|\delta|=n$. In the following, we prove that the conclusion is also correct when$|\delta|=n+1$.

Let $\delta=\delta'\bullet t'$, where t' is the $(n+1)th$ element ofδ and $|\delta'|=n$.

Based on $\delta\in L(W_{CW})$ iff $(M_0[\delta'\bullet t'>M_{n+1})\wedge(M_{n+1}\in M_f)$, $M_0[\delta'>M_n[t'>M_{n+1}$ iff $M_n\subseteq R(M_0)$; and $M_f'=\{M_n|(M_0[\delta'>M_n[t'>M_{n+1})\wedge(M_{n+1}\in M_f)\}$, $M_{fi}'=\{\Delta_{P\to Pi}M_n|M_n\in M_f'\}$ $(i\in\{1, 2, 3...k\})$.

According to the supposition, $\exists\delta_i'=\Pi_{T\to Ti}(\delta')$ and $\delta_i'\in L(W_i)$ such that $\delta_i=\Pi_{T\to Ti}(\delta)=\delta'\bullet t'$ if $t'\in T_i$ and $\delta_i=\Pi_{T\to Ti}(\delta)=\delta'$ otherwise; and $\delta_i\in L(W_i)$ iff $M_{0i}[\delta_i'>M_i'\wedge M_i'\in M_{fi}'$; iff $M_{0i}[\delta_i>M_{(n+1)i}\wedge M_{(n+1)i}\in M_{fi}$, such that $\delta_i\in L(W_i)$ and $\delta_i=\Pi_{T\to Ti}(\delta)$.

Therefore, the theorem is proved.

According to Theorem 5.1, we know that $L(W_{CW})=\Theta_{1\leq i\leq k}L(W_i)$ is the language expression of the cross-organization workflow with task synchronization pattern if the language expression $L(W_i)$ $(i\in\{1, 2, 3...k\})$ of each WF-net can be obtained.

Take the CWF-net of the medical diagnosis cross-organization workflow with synchronous collaboration patterns in Fig. 3 as an example, its language behaviors can be obtained with the above-mentioned approach. Assume that its end place set is defined as $P_f=\{O_1, O_2\}$. Then the behavior description of the W_{CW} in Fig. 3 can be obtained with the following steps:

(1) The language expression of W_S and W_C as shown in Figs. 1-2 are easy to present, which are formally expressed as $L(W_S)=t_1t_2t_3t_4(t_6//t_5t_9t_{10})t_{12}$ and $L(W_C)=t_7t_8t_9t_{10}t_{11}$; and

(2) Based on the Theorem 5.1, the behaviors for the cross-organization medical diagnosis workflow with task synchronization pattern in Fig. 3 can be expressed as $L(W_{CW})=L(W_S)\Theta L(W_C)$, i.e. $L(W_{CW})=(t_1t_2t_3t_4(t_6//t_5t_9t_{10})t_{12})\Theta(t_7t_8t_9t_{10}t_{11})$.

6   Conclusion and Future Work

This paper presents the behavior description approach for a kind cross-organizational workflow with task synchronization pattern using Petri net language, which mainly includes the following three steps: (1) modeling the cross-organizational workflow with task synchronization pattern, we present the CWF-net by extending traditional WF-net; (2) obtaining the behavior expressions of WF-net for each organization; and (3) obtaining the behavior description of the CWF-net using the synchronized shuffle operation of Petri net language.

Currently our approach of behavior description for cross-organizational workflow is limited to the situation with only task with synchronous interaction pattern which belongs to a type of synchronous interaction pattern. In our future work, we will try to extend some of these results for those cross-organizational workflows with both synchronous and asynchronous interaction patterns. In addition, the language expression of CWF-net usually contains "∥" operation, which is difficult to be understood. The simplification method [15] for language expression containing "∥" operation is highly desired in the future.

Acknowledgements. This work was supported in part by NSFC (61472229, 61170079 and 61202152), by the Special Fund for Agro-scientific Research in the Public Interest (201303107), by the Sci. & Tech. Development Fund of Qingdao (13-1-4-153-jch and 2013-1-24), by the open project of the Key Laboratory of Embedded System and Service Computing, Ministry of Education, Tongji University (ESSCKF201403), the Excellent Young Scientist Foundation of Shandong Province (BS2012DX030 and ZR2013FQ030) and the Graduate Innovation Foundation Project of Shandong University of Science and Technology (YC140106).

References

1. Van Der Aalst, W.M.P.: Interorganizational workflows: an approach based on message sequence charts and petri nets. System Analysis and Modeling 34(3), 335–367 (1999)
2. Van Der Aalst, W.M.P.: Process-oriented architectures for electronic commerce and interorganizational workflow. Information Systems 24(8), 639–671 (1999)
3. Van Der Aalst, W.M.P.: Loosely coupled interorganizational workflow: Modeling and analyzing workflows crossing organizational boundaries. Information Management 37, 67–75 (2000)
4. Zeng, Q., Lu, F., Liu, C., Duan, H., Zhou, C.: Modeling and Verification for Cross-department Collaborative Medical Business Processes Using Extended Petri Nets. IEEE Transaction on System, Man and Cybernetics: Systems (forth coming in 2014)
5. Zeng, Q., Sun, S.X., Duan, H., et al.: Cross-organizational collaborative workflow mining from a multi-source log. Decision Support Systems 54(3), 1280–1301 (2013)
6. Liu, C., Zeng, Q., Duan, H., Zhou, M., Lu, F., Cheng, J.: E-Net Modeling and Analysis of Emergency Response Processes Constrained by Resource and Uncertain Durations. IEEE Transaction on System, Man and Cybernetics: Systems (forth coming in 2014)
7. Wang, H., Zeng, Q.: Modeling and Analysis for Workflow Constrained by Resources and Nondetermined Time: An Approach Based on Petri Nets. IEEE Transactions on Systems, Man and Cybernetics, Part A: Systems and Humans 38(4), 802–817 (2008)
8. Zeng, Q., Wang, H., Xu, D., Duan, H., Han, Y.: Conflict detection and resolution for workflows constrained by resources and non-determined durations. Journal of Systems and Software 819, 1491–1504 (2008)
9. Van Der Aalst, W.M.P.: The application of Petri nets to workflow management. Journal of Circuits, Systems, and Computers 8(01), 21–66 (1998)
10. Reisig, W.: Understanding Petri Nets: Modeling Techniques, Analysis Methods, Case Studies. Springer (2013)
11. Murata, T.: Petri nets: Properties, analysis and applications. Proceedings of the IEEE 77(4), 541–580 (1989)

12. Peterson, J.L.: Petri nets. ACM Computing Surveys 9(3), 223–252 (1977)
13. Latteux, M., Roos, Y.: Synchronized shuffle and regular languages. In: Karhumaki, J., Maurer, H.A., Paun, G., Rozenberg, G. (eds.) Jewels are Forever, Contributions on Theoretical Computer Science in Honor of Arto Salomaa, pp. 35–44. Springer (1999) ISBN 3-540-65984-6
14. Zeng, Q., Duan, H.: Behavior description for complex flexible manufacturing system based on decomposition of Petri net. International Journal of Computer Systems Science and Engineering 22(6), 359–363 (2007)
15. Garg, V.K., Raugunath, M.T.: Concurrent regular expressions and their relationships to Petri net. Theoretical Computer Science 96(2), 258–304 (1992)
16. Schulz, K.A., Orlowska, M.E.: Facilitating cross-organisational workflows with a workflow view approach. Data Knowledge Engineering 51(1), 109–147 (2004)
17. Jiang, P., Shao, X., Qiu, H., Li, P.: Interoperability of Cross-organizational Workflows based on Process-view for Collaborative Product Development. Concurrent Engineering 16(1), 73–87 (2008)
18. Yan, C.-G., Jiang, C.-J., Sun, P., Li, Q.-Y.: The Language Study for Workflow Net System Based on Petri Net Reduction Technique. International Journal of Studied in Informatics and Control 15(4), 337–350 (2006)

A New Similarity Search Approach on Process Models

Siyun Li and Jian Cao

Department of CSE, Shanghai Jiao Tong University,
Dongchuan Rd. 800, 200240 Shanghai, China
{lisiyun,cao-jian}@sjtu.edu.cn

Abstract. We investigate the problem of similarity search query in process model repositories: given a certain target model, compare with the process models in the repository and find their similar pattern. We seek to find an effective way to mine out the similar patterns. Using four representative models, we evaluate a new approach, with semantic and topological consideration accordingly. The experimental results show that the combination of semantic and topological analysis brings higher retrieval quality in the similarity search on process models.

Keywords: process model, similarity search, process mining.

1 Introduction

In the large enterprises, their model repositories usually have large number of various process models [1]. In various application scenarios people need to compare process models and retrieve relevant patterns from model repositories. For example, when compressing the model repositories, similarity search enables one to detect the similar and relevant model patterns, which can be extracted out as a shared model component. Meanwhile, the retrieved patterns can be utilized as recommended references when one builds process models. What's more, similarity search helps to figure out the co-relationship of a wide variety of process models across different application domains.

In this paper, we focus on the problem of similarity search query in process model repositories: given a certain target model, compare with the process models in the repository and find out their similar patterns. To tackle this problem, we need to determine the degree of similarity between pairs of models. Previous work has been done for this from several perspectives including text similarity, structural similarity and behavior similarity [2]. However, they are not completely satisfactory in the real-life applications, due to the limit either in the retrieval quality or computational complexity. This paper proposes a new approach with causal similarity mining processes to strike a tradeoff between retrieval quality and computational complexity.

The rest of the paper is structured as follows. Section 2 elaborates the process model notion and similarity metric used in this paper. Section 3 presents the details of two approaches to mine out similar patterns out of process model pairs.

J. Cao et al. (Eds.): PAS 2014, CCIS 495, pp. 11–20, 2015.

Section 4 presents an experimental evaluation of the approaches studied in this paper. Section 5 discusses the related work and Section 6 concludes.

2   Preliminaries

This section defines the notion of process model used in this paper and formulates the similarity metric used for comparing pairs of process models.

2.1   Process Model

A process model consists of a set of related tasks to achieve a certain practical goal. There are several available modeling notations including Event-driven Process Chains (EPC)[3], Business Process Modeling Notation (BPMN)[4] and PetriNet [5]. In this paper, we adopt an abstract view to represent process models from different notations. That a process model is expressed in a directed attributed graph:

Let L be a set of labels. A process model can be defined as a graph $G = (N,E,F)$ where:

- *N is the set of nodes*
- *$E \subset N \times N$, is the set of edges*
- *F: $N \to L$ is a function that maps nodes to labels*

Figure 1 represent four process models in the context of the definition. The legends of Process(a)-(d) are listed in the attached file. They are derived from a process model matching contest [6] and similar to each other for their functionality of describing the birth registration process. Originally these process models are expressed in terms of PetriNet. To be simple, we only capture the active components (i.e., the transitions) rather than the passive ones like places. Also we omit the logical relationship and condition detection among the nodes.

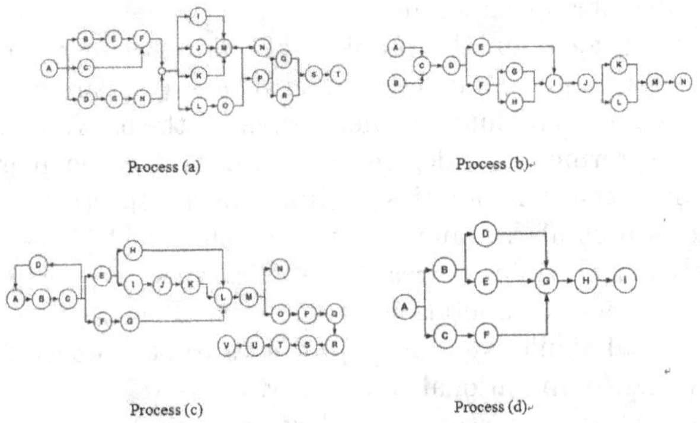

Process (a)

Process (b)

Process (c)

Process (d)

Fig. 1. Process (a)-(d)

As we can see that, processes (a)-(d) are not completely equivalent to one another. Clearly, in real-life applications, it is not that helpful with a binary answer (yes/no for the equivalence) when comparing process models. In the next part, we propose a process similarity metric to determine the degree of similarity and provide a gold standard alignment for the later experimental evaluation.

2.2   Process Similarity Metric

To compare pairs of process models, we define a metric on the semantic and topological basis. In this paper, when a pair of process models contains similar patterns, they should fulfill the following conditions:

Given two graphs $G1(N1,E1,F1)$ and $G2(N2, E2,F2)$, a similar pattern pair is defined as (W,V), where:

- *$W = w1 \bigcup w2 \bigcup ... \bigcup wi \bigcup \{path\ nodes\ between\ wj\ and\ wj+1\}$, where $i = 0,1,2,.., 0 \leq j < i$*
- *$V = v1 \bigcup v2 \bigcup ... \bigcup vi \bigcup \{path\ nodes\ between\ vj\ and\ vj+1\}$, where $i = 0,1,2,.., 0 \leq j < i$*
- *For each pair of correspondence sets(wm, vn), where $0 \leq m,n <$the number of found correspondence sets, we have:*

If $m \neq n$, any nodes in wm has low degree of similarity to any nodes in vn
If $m = n$, the nodes in wm has high degree of similarity to any nodes in vn

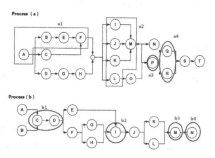

Fig. 2. Standard retrieved pattern from process (a) and (b)

To apply this metric to the models under study in this paper, we select Process (b) as the target model. Next we manually compare each of the three process model pairs and come out with a gold standard alignment for the experimental evaluation part. This manual comparison is done by three students including one doctor.

Figure 2-4 mark with the gold standard summarized in Table 1. Let's look at Figure 2. We have correspondence sets: (a1, b1), (a2, b2), (a3, b3) and (a4, b4). In each correspondence set, any node from the first set is semantic similar to any node from the second set. These correspondence sets are leveraged to formulate the similar pattern between the two process models. By including nodes

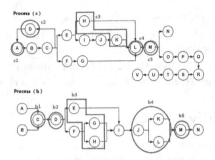

Fig. 3. Standard retrieved pattern from process (c) and (b)

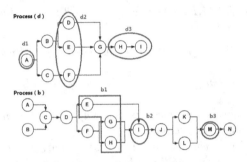

Fig. 4. Standard retrieved pattern from process (d) and (b)

in-between each correspondence set, we figure out the similar pattern in pair of Process (a) and (b) is ($\{a1, a2, a3, a4\}$, $\{b1, \{E, F, G, H\}, b2, \{J, K, L\}, b3, b\}$). Note for calculating the precision rate, we only considers the nodes in the correspondence sets. The rest figures are analog.

Table 1. Gold Standard of Retrieved Patterns

Process model pair	Similar patterns
(a) and (b)	$\{a1, a2, a3, a4\}$ and $\{b1, \{E, F, G, H\}, b2, \{J, K, L\}, b3, b4\}$
(c) and (b)	$\{c1, c2, \{E, I, J\}, c3, c4, c5\}$ and $\{b1, b2, \{F\}, b3, \{I\}, b4, b5\}$
(d) and (b)	$\{d1, \{B, C\}, d2, \{G\}, d3\}$ and $\{b1, b2, \{J, K, L\}, b3\}$

The detail of our proposed approach and its correspondent experimental evaluation is elaborated in the following sections.

3   Approaches

In this paper we propose to mine out similar patterns from pairs of process models via a combinational approach. Before presenting this approach in detail, we first discuss the single straightforward approach.

3.1   Only Consider Semantic Correspondences

In this approach, we compare each process model pair in term of semantic similarity of their labels. We determine the degree of semantic similarity of each label pair by utilizing WordNet [7][8], a powerful lexical database for measuring the relatedness of concepts.

After comparing each label pair we summarize a collection of correspondence sets, in which nodes are similar to each other in view of semantic similarity in labels. Note in this approach we support 1-to-N and N-to-M correspondences.

For example, in case of process model pair (b) and (c), see Figure 3, we figure out five correspondence sets (here the former node set is subset of nodes in process (b) and the later node set is subset of nodes in process (c). The legend is align to Figure 3 accordingly:

Set 1: $(\{C\}, \{A\})$
Set 2: $(\{D\}, \{D\})$
Set 3: $(\{E, G, H\}, \{H, K\})$
Set 4: $(\{J, K, L\}, \{L\})$
Set 5: $(\{M\}, \{M\})$

The patterns in each correspondence set is supposed to be the answer to our similarity search query. For example, $\{J, K, L\}$ in process (b) and L in process (c). Moreover, we can expand the retrieved pattern by assembling patterns when two correspondence sets are adjacent to each other, such as Set 4 and Set 5. As a result, we have our final similar model patterns out of Process (b) and (c): $\{J, K, L, M\}$ and $\{L, M\}$.

3.2   Add Topological Consideration with Adjacency Matrix

Based on the straightforward approach introduced above, we notice that the retrieved result of Approach A strictly depends on the adjacent relation of the correspondence sets. Clearly it is not very helpful in the real-life applications. For example given Process (d) as a target model, we should find $\{E, G, H, I, J, K, L, M\}$ in Process (b) as its similar patterns. However, it is not a valid answer with Approach A.

In addition, there is some limitation when we only compare node labels. Because it leaves out the ordering of activities and more likely results in a scattered distribution of correspondences. In both cases the retrieval quality will be affected.

To address the first problem, we need to take the topology into consideration and differentiate between such $Set1 \rightarrow Set2$ and $Set2 \rightarrow Set1$ case. In this paper, we utilize adjacency matrix [9] to represent the structural properties of the process models under study, where 1 from row i to column j means there is an edge from node i to node j, 0 means there is no edge between them.

When we consider nodes from different correspondence sets, we look up the adjacency matrixes of the process model pair. In this approach we extend the limit of strict adjacent relation between the correspondence sets as below:

Given any n1, m1 from correspondence set 1 and n2, m2 from correspondence set 2, if n1, m1, n2, m2 satisfy: m1 is reachable from n1 and m2 is reachable from n2. Then we consider correspondence set 1 is neighboring to correspondence set 2.

Based on such a rule, we prune the correspondence sets by removing irrelevant nodes from structural perspective and assemble the final retrieved patterns by including the path nodes between correspondence sets.

What's more, in view of the time complexity, looking-up process in adjacency matrixes is far lower than the most graph matching algorithms that are NP-complete [10].

4   Evaluation

In this section, we first analyze the computational complexity and then present an experimental evaluation of the approaches discussed above in terms of the retrieval quality.

4.1   Computational Complexity

The proposed approach involves determining initial correspondence sets, pruning the correspondence sets and assembling the final patterns. In the process of determining the initial correspondence sets, nodes from model N are compared to nodes in model M respectively, which leads to a complexity of $O(n \times m)$, where n,m is the number of nodes in model N and model M. As the basis of our pruning process, we need to construct adjacency matrixes once for all, so its complexity is not our big concern. The pruning process can be carried out via a finite number of look-ups in the adjacency matrixes. One look-up step has complexity of $O(1)$. In the final part, we assembly the final patterns by including the path nodes in-between the correspondence sets. These path nodes are already stored when checking the correspondence sets are reachable to each other.

4.2   Experimental Setup

In this paper, we utilize the four process models shown in Figure 1 as our experimental dataset. On average each model contains 16 nodes with a minimum of 9 and a maximum of 22. We randomly pick up Process (b) as the target model and apply both Approach A and Approach B onto three process model pairs, i.e., Process (a) and (b), Process (c) and (b), Process (d) and (b). In constructing the correspondence sets, we omit those node pair with similarity score lower than half of the highest score in the set.

In the experiment, we applied both approaches to the three process model pairs respectively. The results are recorded in Table 2. With comparison to the gold standard in Figure 2-4, we drew out the retrieval quality of each approach, as shown in Table 3.

4.3   Results

Result of our experiment is summarized in Table 2. We record the retrieved model patterns of both approaches per the process model pairs.

With comparison to the gold standard mentioned in Section 2, we calculated the precision rate of the approaches under study, as shown in Table 3. Precision rate is a measure commonly used to evaluate the quality of search and mining techniques [11].

Table 2. Experimental Result

	Approach A	Approach B
(a) and (b)	$(\{S,T\},\{D,E\})$ or $(\{A,B,E,F,O,J,K\},\{D,E\})$ or $(\{P,Q,R\},\{M,N\})$	$(\{P,Q,R,S,T,A,F,I,J,K,M,D,E\},$ $\{D,E,F,G,H,M,N,I,J,K,L\})$
(c) and (b)	$(\{E,H\},\{F,G\})or(\{E,H\},\{D,E\})$ or $(\{T,U\},\{D,F\})or(\{A,D\},\{D,F\})$	$(\{B,C,D\},\{D,E,F,G\})$
(d) and (b)	$(\{A,B,C,D,E,F,G,H,I\},\{D,E\})$ or $(\{A,B,C,D,E,F,G,H,I\},\{G,H\})$ or $(\{A,B,C,D,E,F,G,H,I\},\{L,M\})$	$(\{A,B,C,D,E,F,G,H,I\},$ $\{F,G,H,I,J,K,L,M\})$

Table 3. Precision of Approach A and Approach B

Approach	(a) and (b)	(c) and (b)	(d) and (b)
Only consider semantic correspondences	0.10344828	0.1369863	0.14285714
Add topological consideration	0.33333333	0.27027027	0.41666667

As we can observe that, given a target model (Process (b) in the experiment), the retrieved results from Approach A are more scattered than the ones from Approach B. Also we see Approach A allows more irrelevant patterns as compared to Approach B. The main reason for that is in Approach A the topological information is omitted, which actually counts a lot when comparing process models. Moreover, due to the strict adjacent relation, we have little merging work done on the correspondence sets. That explains the scattered distribution in the result of Approach A. Clearly, in the real-life application, we need to extend such limit for a more meaningful retrieved result.

In view of the two observations in the experiment on Approach A, we propose Approach B, with loose adjacent relation and topological consideration. The result shows the validity of this optimization, with significantly increased precision rate, as well as the more reasonable retrieved result in comparison with Approach A, as shown in Table 2 and 3.

5   Related Work

Many literatures have targeted in the similarity search of process models. Some propose creative algorithms for measuring the similarity between business process models [12][13][14][15][16]. Some aim at similarity comparison on state machines [17][18]. In [12] a combination of structural properties and label similarity is adopted to compare process models. However it doesn't define an effective fuzzy query metric which is meaningful in the real-life applications. Li [13] compares process models based on the model transformation technique. See [16] a graph edit distance is utilized as the metric for process model comparison. Some focus on the process equivalence and have different judgments. In context of process mining [19], [20] proposes a use of "typical behavior" recorded in event logs. Similar work like equivalence notions, trace equivalence [21] and bi-simulation [22] do not take the syntactical structure into consideration. Moreover, these approaches actually not consider the degree of similarity which is more important in practice. In work of [23], the researchers evaluated several similarity metrics and concluded that a structural similarity metric based on graph matching brings highest retrieval quality. In their follow-up paper [24], four graph matching algorithms are presented. In these algorithms only 1-to-1 correspondences between nodes in the compared process models are established. An improved investigation is shown in [25] that calculate 1-to-N or N-to-M correspondences. Still, all these graph matching algorithms need to strike a tradeoff between the retrieval quality and the time complexity.

This paper is the first to propose a causal similarity search approach by first calculating correspondence sets and pruning on them on the basis of structural properties. In addition, we introduce a fuzzy similarity search metric on model patterns that is more reasonable in practical applications. Moreover, we replace the complex graph traversal process with a series of look-up steps in adjacency matrixes, which reduces the complexity. All these three points make the work different from the references mentioned in this section. What's more, the experimental results show the validity of our approach for mining similar patterns from pair of process models.

6   Conclusion

This paper presented a novel approach to find similar patterns from pairs of process models: a combination of semantic comparison in labels and topological consideration with adjacency matrix for the similarity search on general process models. Also, it introduces a metric of fuzzy similarity search on model patterns which is more reasonable in practical applications. In addition, we convert the traditional graph traversal process to a series look-up steps in adjacency matrixes, which reduces the complexity.

The approach has been tested on a small collection of process models and proved the proposed approach is valid to some extent. However, there is much work to do in the future. For example, the approach still needs further test in large scale of process models or in a wide variety of situations. Also, when coming into complex process models we need to consider the logical relationship. What's more, WordNet is useful only for English words, as for other languages such as Chinese, the method of calculating semantic similarity needs to be revalidated.

Acknowledgments. This work is partially supported by China National Science Foundation (Granted Number 61272438,61472253), Research Funds of Science and Technology Commission of Shanghai Municipality (Granted Number 14511107702, 12511502704).

References

1. Dumas, M., Van der Aalst, W.M.P., Ter Hofstede, A.H.: Process-aware information systems: bridging people and software through process technology. John Wiley & Sons (2005)
2. Dijkman, R., et al.: Similarity of business process models: Metrics and evaluation. Information Systems 36(2), 498–516 (2011)
3. van der Aalst, W.M.P.: Formalization and verification of event-driven process chains. Information and Software Technology 41(10), 639–650 (1999)
4. Mendling, J., Weidlich, M., Weske, M. (eds.): BPMN 2010. LNBIP, vol. 67. Springer, Heidelberg (2010)
5. Reisig, W., Rozenberg, G. (eds.): APN 1998. LNCS, vol. 1491. Springer, Heidelberg (1998)
6. Cayoglu, U., et al.: The Process Model Matching Contest 2013. In: 4th International Workshop on Process Model Collections: Management and Reuse, PMC-MR 2013 (2013)
7. Pedersen, T., Patwardhan, S., Michelizzi, J.: WordNet: Similarity: measuring the relatedness of concepts. In: Demonstration Papers at HLT-NAACL 2004. ACL (2004)
8. Miller, G.A., et al.: Introduction to wordnet: An on-line lexical database*. International Journal of Lexicography 3(4), 235–244 (1990)
9. Godsil, C.D., Royle, G.: Algebraic graph theory. Springer, New York (2001)
10. Messmer, B.T.: Efficient graph matching algorithms (1995)
11. Powers, D.M.: Evaluation: from precision, recall and F-measure to ROC, informedness, markedness and correlation (2011)
12. Ehrig, M., Koschmider, A., Oberweis, A.: Measuring similarity between semantic business process models. In: Proceedings of the Fourth Asia-Pacific Conference on Conceptual Modelling, vol. 67. Australian Computer Society, Inc. (2007)
13. Li, C., Reichert, M., Wombacher, A.: On measuring process model similarity based on high-level change operations. In: Li, Q., Spaccapietra, S., Yu, E., Olivé, A. (eds.) ER 2008. LNCS, vol. 5231, pp. 248–264. Springer, Heidelberg (2008)
14. Lu, R., Sadiq, S.: On the discovery of preferred work practice through business process variants. In: Parent, C., Schewe, K.-D., Storey, V.C., Thalheim, B. (eds.) ER 2007. LNCS, vol. 4801, pp. 165–180. Springer, Heidelberg (2007)
15. Madhusudan, T., Zhao, J.L., Marshall, B.: A case-based reasoning framework for workflow model management. Data & Knowledge Engineering 50(1), 87–115 (2004)
16. Minor, M., Tartakovski, A., Bergmann, R.: Representation and structure-based similarity assessment for agile workflows. In: Weber, R.O., Richter, M.M. (eds.) ICCBR 2007. LNCS (LNAI), vol. 4626, pp. 224–238. Springer, Heidelberg (2007)

17. Nejati, S., et al.: Matching and merging of statecharts specifications. In: Proceedings of the 29th International Conference on Software Engineering. IEEE Computer Society (2007)
18. Wombacher, A.: Evaluation of technical measures for workflow similarity based on a pilot study. In: Meersman, R., Tari, Z. (eds.) OTM 2006. LNCS, vol. 4275, pp. 255–272. Springer, Heidelberg (2006)
19. Van der Aalst, W.M.P., Weijters, T., Maruster, L.: Workflow mining: Discovering process models from event logs. IEEE Transactions on Knowledge and Data Engineering 16(9), 1128–1142 (2004)
20. van der Aalst, W.M.P., de Medeiros, A.K.A., Weijters, A.J.M.M.: Process equivalence: Comparing two process models based on observed behavior. In: Dustdar, S., Fiadeiro, J.L., Sheth, A.P. (eds.) BPM 2006. LNCS, vol. 4102, pp. 129–144. Springer, Heidelberg (2006)
21. Van Glabbeek, R.J., Weijland, W.P.: Branching time and abstraction in bisimulation semantics. Journal of the ACM (JACM) 43(3), 555–600 (1996)
22. Milner, R. (ed.): A calculus of communicating systems, vol. 92. Springer, Heidelberg (1980)
23. van Dongen, B., Dijkman, R., Mendling, J.: Measuring similarity between business process models. In: Bellahsène, Z., Léonard, M. (eds.) CAiSE 2008. LNCS, vol. 5074, pp. 450–464. Springer, Heidelberg (2008)
24. Dijkman, R., Dumas, M., García-Bañuelos, L.: Graph matching algorithms for business process model similarity search. In: Dayal, U., Eder, J., Koehler, J., Reijers, H.A. (eds.) BPM 2009. LNCS, vol. 5701, pp. 48–63. Springer, Heidelberg (2009)
25. Ambauen, R., Fischer, S., Bunke, H.: Graph edit distance with node splitting and merging, and its application to diatom identification. In: Hancock, E.R., Vento, M. (eds.) IAPR Workshop GbRPR 2003. LNCS, vol. 2726, pp. 95–106. Springer, Heidelberg (2003)

Workflow Scheduling in Grid
Based on Bacterial Foraging Optimization

Feng Yao[1,2,3], Jidong Ge [1,2,3,*], Chuanyi Li[1,2,3], Yuhang Ge[1,2,3], Haiyang Hu[1,2,4],
Yu Zhou[1,5], Hao Hu[1], and Bin Luo[1,2]

[1] State Key Laboratory for Novel Software Technology, Software Institute,
Nanjing University, Nanjing, China, 210093
gjdnju@163.com
[2] State Key Laboratory of Networking and Switching Technology
(Beijing University of Posts and Telecommunications), Beijing, China, 100876
[3] Key Laboratory of Intelligent Perception and Systems for High-Dimensional Information,
Ministry of Education, Nanjing University of Science and Technology, Nanjing, China, 210094
[4] School of Computer, Hangzhou Dianzi University, Hangzhou, China, 310018
[5] College of Computer Science, Nanjing University of Aeronautics and Astronautics,
Nanjing, China, 210016

Abstract. Optimal assignment of a workflow application in heterogeneous computing system is NP-complete in general case. We proposed the algorithm based on bacterial foraging optimization technique for Grid resource scheduling. This algorithm aims at minimizing the makespan of workflow application. To show the advantage of this algorithm, we made comparison with ant colony optimization and particle swarm optimization. The experiment shows that this bacterial foraging optimization algorithm is better than the other two algorithms in minimizing the makespan.

Keywords: Workflow scheduling, Grid computing, Bacterial foraging optimization.

1   Introduction

Grid computing is the collection of computer resource from multiple locations to reach a common goal. The main characteristics of grid computing are loosely coupled, heterogeneous, and geographically dispersed. Task scheduling subsystem is the core part of grid computing. Task scheduling subsystem assigns all tasks with the corresponding resources based on the application requirement.

Grid applications are basically categorized into two types [2]; meta-task application and DAG application. The former one describes independent tasks which have no priority relations and data dependences among them. The latter one is known as workflow application which is represented as Directed Acyclic Graph (DAG), in which the nodes of the graph have dependences between them. The quality of a

---

* Corresponding author.

J. Cao et al. (Eds.): PAS 2014, CCIS 495, pp. 21–34, 2015.
© Springer-Verlag Berlin Heidelberg 2015

scheduling plan can be measured using several optimization criteria, such as minimizing the makespan (the completion time of the last task), meeting the deadline, or within the budget. In this research, we consider the DAG application scheduling problem with the most commonly used criteria, i.e. minimizing the makespan.

The goal of mapping tasks on grid resources has been proven to be NP-complete [1]. In recent years, people have proposed a lot of heuristic algorithms and meta-heuristic algorithm to solve this problem. Heuristic algorithms contain Min-min, Max-min, Sufferage [3], XSufferage [4], Segemented Min-min [5], Qos Guided Min-min [6], HEFT [7], etc. Meta-heuristic algorithm can also be applied to solve the problem, such as Greedy Randomized Adaptive Search Process (GRASP) [8], Genetic Algorithm (GA) [9], Simulated Annealing (SA) [10], Ant Colony Optimization [14], Particle Swarm Optimization [15]. Jia Yu [11] provided a more detailed overview of workflow scheduling problem solution.

The Bacterial Foraging Optimization (BFO) algorithm [12] was proposed by Passino et al. It is a population-based numerical optimization algorithm based on foraging behavior of Escherichia coli bacteria. In paper [13], they use Bacterial Foraging Optimization to resource scheduling in grid computing. However, they are dealing with meta-task scheduling problem.

In this paper, we proposed a workflow scheduling algorithm based on Bacterial Foraging Optimization. This algorithm aims at minimizing the makespan of a workflow application. The experiment shows that the approach proposed is effective to solve task scheduling problem in grid workflow application.

The rest of this paper is organized as follows. Section 2 formalizes the task scheduling problem in grid workflow application. Section 3 introduces the task scheduling optimization process based on Bacterial Foraging Optimization. Section 4 uses the experiment to evaluate the approach proposed in this paper with other algorithms. Section 5 draws a conclusion.

2   Problem Statement

Workflow application is composed by many interrelate tasks. Viewing each task as a node, communication and precedence constraints between tasks as a directed edge, the grid application can be expressed as a Directed Acyclic Graph (DAG).

Definition 1. (Workflow Application) workflow application can be represented as a quad, $WF = (T, E, D, C)$, T is set of tasks, E is the set of edges between tasks, E_{ij} means the edges from task T_i to task T_j. $D = \{d_1, d_2, d_3, ..., d_n\}$ is the workload of each task. C is the communication data between tasks. C_{ij} means the communication data from task T_i to task T_j.

Without loss of generality, we assume one entry and exit task. The set of parent tasks is denoted as $pred(T_i)$, the set of children tasks is denoted as $succ(T_i)$. A task T_i is called entry task if $|pred(T_i)| = 0$, and an exit task if $|succ(T_i)| = 0$.

An example workflow application is showed in Fig. 1. The number in the circle denotes the task name. The edges between the circles mean the tasks have communication dependencies.

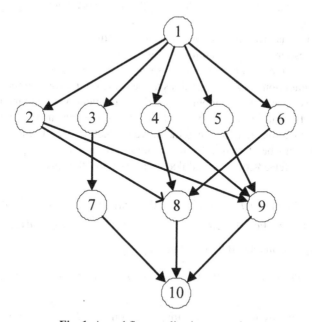

Fig. 1. A workflow application example

Definition 2 (Grid Resource) grid resource is triple, $GR = (M, R, X)$, M is the set of resources, $R = \{r_1, r_2, r_3, ..., r_m\}$ is the calculating speed of grid resources. X is a $m \times m$ matrix, X_{ij} is the bandwidths between resource M_i and M_j. A grid resource example is showed in Fig. 2.

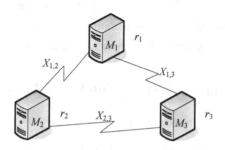

Fig. 2. A grid resource example

When scheduling a workflow to grid resources, it has to satisfy following conditions:

1. Every task can be scheduled to any grid resource. The execution time of a task is determined by workload of the task and calculating speed of grid resource.
2. Every task is processed on one resource at a time.
3. Every resource processes only one task at a time.
4. Grid resource is connected in a strongly connected topology in which all communication between resources are assumed to perform without contention
5. Grid resource can do computation and communication simultaneously.
6. When two tasks are scheduled to the same resources and they have communications data between them, we neglect the communication time.
7. A task can't be started until the communication data of all parent tasks have been transferred to the scheduled resources and the resources must be in the idle state.

We use $ST(T_i)$ and $FT(T_i)$ to denote the start time of task T_i and end time of task T_i respectively. For the entry task T_{entry}, $ST(T_{entry}) = 0$. Given a scheduling scheme, $ST(T_i)$ is calculated by formula (1)

$$ST(T_i) = \max\{avail(M_k), \max_{T_j \in pred(T_i)} (FT(T_j) + C_{i,j}/s)\} \qquad (1)$$

$avail(M_k)$ denotes the available time of resource M_k, $pred(T_i)$ is the set of immediate predecessor of task T_i, $C_{i,j}$ is communication data size, s is bandwidth between resources. The equation means the start time of task T_i is the maximum of resource available time and the time when all precede data have been transferred to the resource. $FT(T_i)$ is calculated by formula (2).

$$FT(T_i) = d_i/r + ST(T_i) \qquad (2)$$

d_i is the workload of task T_i, r is the calculating speed of grid resource. After all tasks have been scheduled, the finish time of exit task T_{exit} is recorded as the makespan of workflow application. This paper aims at minimizing the makespan.

3   Bacterial Foraging Optimization Based Algorithm

3.1   Bacterial Foraging Optimization

Bacterial Foraging Optimization algorithm is a population-based numerical optimization algorithm proposed by Passino [12]. It simulated the foraging behavior of Escherichia coli bacteria. Foraging is a process in which a group of bacteria move in search of food in a region. Bacteria search for nutrient in a manner to maximize energy obtained per unit time. There are four basic steps of bacteria foraging optimization: Chemotaxis, Swarming, Reproduction and Elimination-dispersal. The variables that used in the formula are explained in following.

j : index for the chemotactic step

k : index for reproduction step

l : index of the elimination-dispersal step

p : dimension of the search space

S : total number of bacteria in the population

N_c : the number of chemotactic steps

N_s : the swimming length

N_{re} : the number of reproduction steps

N_{ed} : the number of elimination-dispersal events

P_{ed} : elimination-dispersal probability

$C(i)$: the size of step taken in the random location specified by the tumble

Chemotaxis: This simulates the movement of E.coli bacteria through swimming and tumbling via flagella. Swim means the bacterial cells move in the same direction. Tumble means the bacterial cells move in a random direction. The bacterial cells alternate between swim and tumble for the entire lifetime. The tumble movement is formulated as follow:

$$\theta^i(j+1,k,l) = \theta^i(j,k,l) + C(i)\phi(j) \tag{3}$$

$\theta^i(j,k,l)$ denotes the current position of the ith individual at the jth chemotaxis step, k^{th} reproduction step and l^{th} elimination-dispersal events. $\phi(j)$ is a random direction angle of the jth chemotaxis step.

If the cost at $\theta^i(j+1,k,l)$ is better than the cost at $\theta^i(j,k,l)$, the bacterium will swim another step of size $C(i)$ in the same direction as the tumble movement did, otherwise it is allowed to tumble in a random direction $\theta(j)$. The process is repeated until the number of maximum swimming length N_s is reached.

Swarming: Cell-released attractants are used to signal other cells that they should swarm together. The cell also repels a nearby cell in the sense that it consumes nearby nutrients and it is not physically possible to have two cells at the same locations. Thus all cells will have a cell to cell attraction via attractant and cell to cell repulsion via repellant. The cell to cell signaling in E.coli swarm is representing as formula (4):

$$J_{cc}(\theta, p(j,k,l)) =$$

$$\sum_{i=1}^{S} J_{cc}(\theta, \theta^i(j,k,l)) = \sum_{i=1}^{S} [d_{attractant} \exp(w_{attractant} \sum_{m=1}^{p} (\theta_m - \theta_m^i)^2)] +$$

$$\sum_{i=1}^{S} [h_{repellant} \exp(w_{repellant} \sum_{m=1}^{p} (\theta_m - \theta_m^i)^2)] \tag{4}$$

$J_{cc}(\theta, p(j,k,l))$ means the objective function value to be added to actual objective functions. The sum of $J_{cc}(\theta, p(j,k,l))$ and $J(j,k,l)$ is called as fitness value which represent how much nutrient that bacterium detected, the accumulated fitness value denotes the health level of bacterial which will be used in reproduction step to discarded the unhealthy bacterium. The whole formula denotes the combined cell-to-cell attraction and repelling effects, where $\theta = [\theta_1, \theta_2, ..., \theta_p]$ is a position in optimization domain and θ_m^i is the mth component of the ith bacterium at position θ^i. $d_{attractant}$ is the depth of attractant released by the cell and $w_{attractant}$ is a measure of the width of the attractant signal. $h_{repellant}$ is the height of the repellant effect and $w_{repellant}$ is a measure of the width of the repellant. $h_{repellant}$ is often chose as the same value of $d_{attractant}$.

Reproduction: After N_c chemotaxis steps, a reproduction step is taken. First the bacteria are sorted by the accumulated fitness value in an ascending order. The half bacteria which have the higher fitness value are discarded. The other half bacteria are asexually split into two bacteria which are then placed in the same direction. The whole process makes the swarm size constant.

Elimination and dispersal: Bacteria may die due to some sudden changes like significant local rise of temperature. P_{ed} is the elimination-dispersal probability. The eliminated bacteria are often randomly placed in the optimization domain.

3.2   The Proposed Algorithm

In this section, we present the bacteria foraging optimization algorithm to solve workflow scheduling in Grid environment. Each bacterium is a solution to the workflow scheduling problem. The objective of the BFO is to find the bacterium which has the minimum makespan.

3.2.1   Bacterial Representation and Initial Position Generation

One key issue when designing the BFO algorithm lies in its solution representation where the bacteria bear the necessary information related to the problem domain. For workflow scheduling problem, an intermediate representation is obtained as following. The bacterium is encoded with a scheduling vector and allocation matrix. The scheduling vector indicated the scheduling sequence of all tasks. The allocation matrix defined the mapping between tasks to grid resources. The scheduling vector is a permutation of task number, beside it needs to follow the restriction of DAG. Given tasks $T = \{T_1, T_2, ..., T_n\}$, the scheduling vector can be denoted as follows.

$$SV = \{T_{k1}, T_{k2}, ..., T_{kn}\} \tag{5}$$

Every task number is presented in the scheduling vector and appears only once. The scheduling vector specified the scheduling order of the workflow application. The initial scheduling vector can be generated using a breath-first search procedure over the workflow DAG.

Suppose tasks $T = \{T_1, T_2, ..., T_n\}$, resources $M = \{M_1, M_2, ..., M_m\}$, the allocation matrix can expressed as follows.

$$AM = \begin{vmatrix} am_{1,1} & am_{1,2} & \cdots & am_{1,m} \\ am_{2,1} & am_{2,2} & \cdots & am_{2,m} \\ \cdots & \cdots & \ddots & \cdots \\ am_{n,1} & am_{n,2} & \cdots & am_{n,m} \end{vmatrix} \tag{6}$$

Here $am_{i,j}$ denotes the possibility that task T_i will be executed on resource M_j. The allocation matrix's value is initially picked up from a uniformed distributed value in the interval [0, 1]. The value of allocation matrix has to satisfy the following conditions:

$$am_{i,j} \in [0,1]\, i \in \{1,2,...,n\}, j \in \{1,2,...,m\} \tag{7}$$

$$\sum_{j=1}^{m} am_{i,j} = 1\, i \in \{1,2,...,n\}, j \in \{1,2,...,m\} \tag{8}$$

Formula (7) means that the value of allocation matrix is between 0 and 1. So when the value of allocation matrix exceeds the value boundary, we set the value to the nearest boundary value. Formula (8) represents that the sum of all possibility value of allocates T_i to resources is 1. When updating the allocation matrix value, formula (8) could be violated, so we normalize the allocation matrix to satisfy the condition. The normalize process is showed in formula (9).

$$am_{i,j} = \frac{am_{i,j}}{\sum_{k=1}^{m} am_{i,k}} \tag{9}$$

When deciding which resource the task T_i will be scheduled on, we choose the resources with the maximum possibility.

$$m_j = \max(am_{i,j})\ j \in \{1,2,...,m\} \tag{10}$$

3.2.2   Objective Function

In BFO algorithm, all bacterial at each iteration step are evaluated according to a measure of solution quality. Here we use makespan as the objective function. Given a bacteria's scheduling vector and allocation matrix, the bacteria can be evaluated according to formula (1) and (2), while the best bacterial position is saved.

3.2.3   Update Bacteria

The position of a bacterium consists of two parts, namely scheduling vector and allocation matrix. Allocation matrix can use formula (3) to updates itself during the chemotaxis step. Scheduling vector can't use formula (3) to updates itself during the chemotaxis step because the updated scheduling vector may not be a feasible scheduling vector. We adopt the crossover operation in the Genetic Algorithm [9] to construct a new scheduling vector. It has been approved that if the two scheduling vectors are both feasible scheduling vector, then the newly constructed scheduling vector is valid scheduling vector through crossover operation [9].

The crossover operation randomly chooses other bacterium's scheduling vector to form a pair of scheduling vector. For each pair, it randomly generates a cut-off point, which divides the scheduling vector of the pair into the first part and the second part. Then the subtasks in each second part are reordered. The new ordering of the subtasks in one's second part is the relative position of these subtasks in the other original scheduling vector in the pair. Fig. 3 demonstrates such a scheduling vector crossover process given the workflow graph in Fig. 1.

SV_1	1	3	4	5	6	2	8	7	9	10
SV_2	1	4	3	2	5	9	6	8	7	10

Cut-off index is 4 (start from 0)

SV_1^{new}	1	3	4	5	2	9	6	8	7	10
SV_2^{new}	1	4	3	2	5	6	8	7	9	10

Fig. 3. A scheduling vector crosses over example

Because scheduling vector is discrete value, the swarm effects doesn't consider the scheduling vector.

3.2.4   The Bacterial Foraging Algorithm

After defined the solution representation, we provide the BFO based scheduling heuristic. BFO algorithm provide mapping of the entire task to a set of given resource based on the model described in section 2.The pseudo code of our bacterial foraging algorithm is given in Algorithm 1.

```
Algorithm 1: BFO based scheduling heuristic

Input: workflow application model WF, grid resource GR

Output: schedule all tasks to resources and minimize
the makespan of workflow application

Parameter:

S: the number of bacteria in the population

C(i): the size of the step taken in the random direction
specified by the tumble
```

N_c: chemotaxis steps

N_s: swimming length

N_{re}: reproduction steps

N_{ed}: elimination and dispersal events

P_{ed}: elimination and dispersal probability

The algorithm:

1) Calculate computation cost of all task on all grid resource.

2) Calculate cost of communication data that transmitted between different grid resource (tasks that are scheduled to the same grid resource doesn't have communication cost).

3) Initialize the scheduling vector and allocation matrix for each bacterial.

4) Elimination and dispersal loop $l = l+1$

5) Reproduction loop $k = k+1$

6) Chemotaxis loop $j = j+1$

7) For $i = 1,2,3...,S$ take a chemotaxis step for bacterium i as follow

    a) Calculate objective function $J(j,k,l)$,

$$J(j,k,l) = J(i, j,k,l) + J_{cc}(am^i(j,k,l), P(j,k,l))$$

    b) Let $J_{fit} = J(i, j,k,l)$ to save the current fitness value

    c) Tumble: Generate a random direction $\varphi(i)$, which the value is between interval $[-1,1]$

    d) Move: Let $am^i(j+1,k,l) = am^i(j,k,l) + C(i)\phi(i)$, this results in a step of size $C(i)$ in the direction of the tumble for bacterium i. Normalize $am^i(j+1,k,l)$ according to formula (9).

e) Calculate $J(i,j+1,k,l)$,

$$J(i,j+1,k,l)=J(i,j+1,k,l)+J_{cc}(am^i(j+1,k,l),p(j+1,k,l)).$$

f) swim: let $m=0$ (counter for swim length)

    While $m<N_s$

      If $J(i,j+1,k,l)<J_{fit}$ (if doing better), let
$J_{fit}=J(i,j+1,k,l)$ and let

$$am^i(j+1,k,l)=am^i(j+1,k,l)+C(i)\phi(i)$$

      And use this $am^i(j+1,k,l)$ to calculate the
new $J(i,j+1,k,l)$ as step e) did

    Else, let $m=N_s$, this is the end of this while
statement.

g) Scheduling vector update: randomly choose a
scheduling vector from the population of
bacterium; generate a new scheduling vector
through crossover operation. Calculate the new
objective function $J_{new}(j,k,l)$, if $J_{new}(j,k,l)<J_{last}(j,k,l)$,
update the scheduling vector.

8) if $j<N_c$, go to step 6, continue chemotaxis step.

9) Reproduction:

h) For the given k and l, and for each $i\in 1,2,...,S$,
let $J^i_{health}=\sum_{j=1}^{N_c+1}J(i,j,k,l)$ be the health of bacterium i (a
measure of how many nutrient it got over its
lifetime and how successful it was at avoiding
noxious substances). Here in workflow scheduling
problem J^i_{health} denotes the accumulated makespan
value during the bacterium lifetime. Sort bacteria
in order of ascending cost J_{health}.

i) The half bacteria with higher J_{health} values die
and the other half bacteria are split (and the
copies that are made are placed at the same
location as their parent).

10) if $k < N_{re}'$, go to step 5, we start next generation in the chemotactic loop

11) Elimination-dispersal: for $i = 1,2,...,S$ with probability p_{ed}, eliminate and disperse each bacterium (this keeps the number of bacteria in the population constant). When eliminate a bacterium, we disperse it to a random location on the optimization domain.

12) if $l < N_{ed}$, then go to step 4; otherwise end.

4 Experimental Evaluations

The proposed BFO-based algorithm for workflow scheduling was implemented in java programming language on an i3 3.07GHz, 4GB RAM machine running under windows 7. To measure the performance of proposed BFO-based algorithm, we compare our algorithm with ant colony algorithm [14] and partial swarm optimization [15].

The parameter settings for the algorithms are showed in Table 1.

Table 1. Parameter settings for the algorithm (ACO, PSO, BFO)

Algorithm	Parameter name	Parameter Value
ACO	Maximum loop number	50
	Ant number	50
	History coefficient	1.2
	Heuristic coefficient	1
	Decay factor	0.1
PSO	Swarm size	50
	Self-recognition coefficient	2
	Social coefficient	2
	Inertial weight	0.9
BFO	Population size	50
	Elimination-dispersal steps	2
	Reproduction steps	4
	Chemotaxis steps	70
	Maximum swim steps	4
	Step size	0.1
	Elimination-dispersal probability	0.25
	Attraction depth	0.1
	Attraction width	0.2
	Repellant depth	0.1
	Repellant width	10

For every algorithm, we have done eight sets of experiments and every experiment was repeated 10 times with random seed. The task number of workflow DAG graph ranged from 20 to 160. The resource number is fixed as 10. The computation cost of each task was randomly selected from a normal distribution, so as the communication data size between tasks. We assume the resources are fully connected and their computation capacities are randomly selected from a normal distribution. The makespan value of the best solutions through the optimization run was recorded and the average makespan was calculated from the 10 different trials. The average time of each algorithm to generate the optimal solution was also recorded. The percentage of improvement in makespan for BFO algorithm is calculated as formula [11]:

$$\delta = (1 - \frac{\sum Makespan^{avg}{}_{BFO}}{\sum Makespan^{avg}{}_{other}}) \times 100 \tag{11}$$

Table 2 shows the performance comparisons of the three algorithms. M_{best} denotes the best makespan value of the ten trials. M_{avg} denotes the average makespan of the ten trials. T_{avg} denotes the average execution time to get a optimal solution for each algorithm. The three variables are all measured in seconds.

Table 2. Comparison of results for different tasks (s)

Tasks	ACO			PSO			BFO		
	M_{best}	M_{avg}	T_{avg}	M_{best}	M_{avg}	T_{avg}	M_{best}	M_{avg}	T_{avg}
20	98.1	106.6	0.1	102.7	104.2	2.1	91.6	91.8	3.0
40	172.8	194.8	0.6	172.8	174.9	4.4	161.7	162.4	5.0
60	233.5	247.2	1.4	216.0	217.7	6.5	207.1	213.2	6.4
80	314.4	326.0	3.3	292.4	298.9	9.3	277.0	278.4	7.8
100	420.3	432.7	8.5	387.1	387.4	11.0	376.8	382.4	9.4
120	475.6	504.4	12.0	421.5	425.6	14.0	419.4	421.9	11.1
140	574.5	602.5	20.4	500.5	513.2	16.2	498.4	508.8	12.4
160	695.6	719.7	33.5	594.3	597.3	17.3	593.6	596.3	13.9

It is observed that the BFO-based algorithm show better performance than ACO and PSO with the improvement of 11.8% and 3.1% in average makespan. According to the Table 2, we compare the execution time in Figure 4.

It is observed that the execution time of PSO and BFO algorithm is linearly increased as the task increased, while the execution time of ACO algorithm increased drastically. When the task number is below 60, ACO and PSO algorithm takes less time to generate an optimal solution. When the number exceeds 60, the BFO algorithm takes less time to generate an optimal solution than PSO method.

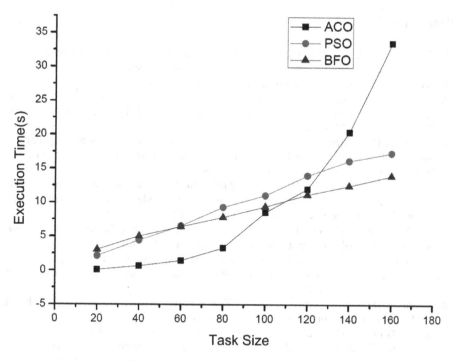

Fig. 4. Execution time of each algorithm

5   Conclusions

In this paper, we analyzed the workflow scheduling problem on computational grids. We proposed bacterial foraging based algorithm to solve the problem. We used an intermediate representation for the scheduling solution. The proposed approach is to generate an optimal schedule so as to complete the workflow in minimum period of time. We evaluated the performance of bacterial foraging algorithm and compared the performance with ant colony algorithm and particle swarm optimization. BFO based method outperforms other algorithm in minimizing the makespan and it takes less execution time to get the optimal solution when the workflow task size becomes large.

Acknowledgments. This work was supported by the National Natural Science Foundation, China (No.61100039, 61021062, 61272188, 91318301), the 973 Program (2009CB320702), the Natural Science Foundation of Jiangsu Province (No.BK20131277), the Fund of State Key Laboratory for Novel Software Technology (Nanjing University), the Open Foundation of State key Laboratory of Networking and Switching Technology (Beijing University of Posts and Telecommunications) (SKLNST-2013-1-14).

References

1. Fernández-Baca, D.: Allocating modules to processors in a distributed system. IEEE Transactions on Software Engineering 15(11), 1427–1436 (1989)
2. Sinnen, O.: Task scheduling for parallel systems. John Wiley & Sons (2007)
3. Maheswaran, M., Ali, S., Siegel, H.J., et al.: Dynamic mapping of a class of independent tasks onto heterogeneous computing systems. Journal of Parallel and Distributed Computing 59(2), 107–131 (1999)
4. Casanova, H., Legrand, A., Zagorodnov, D., et al.: Heuristics for scheduling parameter sweep applications in grid environments. In: Proceedings of 9th Heterogeneous Computing Workshop (HCW 2000), pp. 349–363. IEEE Press, New York (2000)
5. Wu, M.Y., Shu, W., Zhang, H.: Segmented min-min: A static mapping algorithm for meta-tasks on heterogeneous computing systems. In: Proceedings of 9th Heterogeneous Computing Workshop (HCW 2000), pp. 375–375. IEEE Press, New York (2000)
6. He, X.S., Sun, X.H., Von Laszewski, G.: QoS guided min-min heuristic for grid task scheduling. Journal of Computer Science and Technology 18(4), 442–451 (2003)
7. Topcuoglu, H., Hariri, S., Wu, M.: Performance-effective and low-complexity task scheduling for heterogeneous computing. IEEE Transactions on Parallel and Distributed Systems 13(3), 260–274 (2002)
8. Blythe, J., Jain, S., Deelman, E., et al.: Task scheduling strategies for workflow-based applications in grids. In: Proceedings of International Symposium on Cluster Computing and the Grid 2005 (CCGrid 2005), pp. 759–767. IEEE Press, New York (2005)
9. Wang, L., Siegel, H.J., Roychowdhury, V.P., et al.: Task matching and scheduling in heterogeneous computing environments using a genetic-algorithm-based approach. Journal of Parallel and Distributed Computing 47(1), 8–22 (1997)
10. Young, L., McGough, S., Newhouse, S., et al.: Scheduling architecture and algorithms within the ICENI Grid middleware. In: Proceedings of UK e-Science All Hands Meeting, pp. 5–12 (2003)
11. Yu, J., Buyya, R., Ramamohanarao, K.: Workflow scheduling algorithms for grid computing. In: Xhafa, F., Abraham, A. (eds.) Meta. for Sched. in Distri. Comp. Envi. SCI, vol. 146, pp. 173–214. Springer, Heidelberg (2008)
12. Passino, K.M.: Biomimicry of bacterial foraging for distributed optimization and control. IEEE Control Systems 22(3), 52–67 (2002)
13. Chana, I.: Bacterial foraging based hyper-heuristic for resource scheduling in grid computing. Future Generation Computer Systems 29(3), 751–762 (2013)
14. Fidanova, S., Durchova, M.: Ant algorithm for grid scheduling problem. In: Lirkov, I., Margenov, S., Waśniewski, J. (eds.) LSSC 2005. LNCS, vol. 3743, pp. 405–412. Springer, Heidelberg (2006)
15. Liu, H., Abraham, A., Hassanien, A.E.: Scheduling jobs on computational grids using a fuzzy particle swarm optimization algorithm. Future Generation Computer Systems 26(8), 1336–1343 (2010)

Research on Workflow Scheduling Algorithms in the Cloud

Congyang Chen[1,2], Jianxun Liu[1,2], Yiping Wen[1,2], and Jinjun Chen[1,2,3]

[1] Key Laboratory of Knowledge Processing and Networked Manufacture,
Hunan University of Science and Technology, Xiangtan, China
[2] School of Computer Science & Engineering,
Hunan University of Science and Technology, Xiangtan, China
[3] Faculty of Engineering and Information Technology,
University of Technology, Sydney, Australia
chencongyangmm@gmail.com

Abstract. Cloud computing owns merits of more efficiency and less cost in fields of information processing and service mode. Algorithms of workflow scheduling in the cloud can contribute to cutting cost and improving the quality of services, therefore, it has been a hot research topic. In this paper, the workflow technology in the cloud and the needs for cloud workflow scheduling are firstly introduced. Then, typical cloud workflow scheduling algorithms are analyzed and classified into three categories. In the end, typical cloud workflow scheduling research tools such as CloudSim, WorkflowSim and SwinFlow-Cloud are evaluated. Besides, we also analyze the existing problems of current workflow scheduling algorithm in the cloud and introduce the directions of the future research.

Keywords: Cloud computing, Workflow, Scheduling algorithm, CloudSim.

1   Introduction

With the promotion of the world's leading companies, cloud computing has achieved significant developments and applications in recent years. Cloud computing can be defined as the epitome of distributed computing, parallel computing, utility computing, pervasive computing and grid computing. We can obtain data storage which it is security, convenient, efficient, and huge amounts of computer power based on the Internet. Regarded as a distributed computing paradigm with rapid growth, it has shown some obvious difference with other. In this regard, the running environment is controlled by user/application program in cloud environment; always the jobs in user level will not be exposed to the scheduling system, the VM will be allocated to users or none. In brief, cloud computing environment provides three forms of services, they are Infrastructure as a Service (IaaS), Platform as a Service (PaaS) and Software as a Service(SaaS), which can offer the flexible payment services [1,2]. It can satisfy the various requires of services and bring the possibility of service innovations [3] It also has made great strides in developing cloud computing simulation tools. Many cloud computing platforms are also implemented by some famous corporations.

J. Cao et al. (Eds.): PAS 2014, CCIS 495, pp. 35–48, 2015.

Now, a series of problems are exposed with the extensively developed and further used in cloud computing, of which the most outstanding one is how to reduce cost and meanwhile keep or improve the QoS, at last maximize the revenues. Workflow technology can support business process management and business process automation, and enhance flexibility of business process system and the ability of fitting for change. Therefore, it can be used to solve such problems. Generally speaking, by using workflow technology, the business process can be resolved to some manageable small events, and individually model and control the procedural semantics which describe constraint relation between activities. A workflow application can be described by a directed acyclic graph, the nodes denote tasks and the edges denote the internal dependency between activities. Single workflow always contains a series of tasks, and each task may communicate with other task because of the dependency.

A workflow management system (WfMS) can manage the definition and execution control of business processes. Workflow engine is the key component of a WfMS to manage workflow's execution, which can be used to perform workflow scheduling, data transmission and fault tolerance management. The aim of workflow scheduling is to assign appropriate task to the right resource at appropriate time. Data transmission is used for the communication between data resources, and fault tolerance management works when the execution of some task goes wrong. Workflow scheduling is the most critical for a WfMS, because an appropriate scheduling plan has a significant impact on performance of WfMS.

This paper focuses on the typical cloud workflow scheduling algorithms and typical tools for its research. The rest of the paper is organized as follows. Section 2 briefly introduces the state-of-art of workflow technology and its technical features in cloud. Section 3 analyzes various existing workflow scheduling algorithms and classified them into three categories. Section 4 evaluates typical research tools such as CloudSim, WorkflowSim and SwinFlow-Cloud. Section 5 analyzes the problems of current workflow scheduling algorithms in the cloud and proposes the improvement direction. Section 6 concludes the paper.

2   Workflow Technology in Cloud Environment

The promising cloud computing environment brings new challenges to the traditional workflow technology. The research on cloud workflow aims at deploying the business process specified by user automatically in cloud, so that can reduce computational expense and improve the quality of cloud services. It integrates the technical advantages of cloud computing and the workflow system, so regarded as one of optimization solutions for cloud computing, it has been obtained more and more attention and study.

Using workflow technology in the cloud can take advantage of various cloud services which facilitate execution of workflow greatly. Unlike other computing environments, the resource in cloud is shared and offered to user on demand, meanwhile, also can use the resource dynamically according to the estimated requirements of execution. It makes workflow system satisfy the request of applications more easily.

In addition cloud services are mostly expensive for computing, storage and bandwidth, etc. The business model of pay as you go also can reduce the cost of workflow execution [4, 5]. Therefore, optimization of the workflow execution in cloud computing has become one of the research hotspots in the research of workflow and cloud computing recently.

Generally speaking, it is necessary to map tasks to the appropriate execution resource by some workflow scheduling algorithms in cloud, which will directly influence the success rate of cloud workflow scheduling and the execution efficiency. Besides, unlike traditional workflow scheduling, cloud workflow scheduling should consider not only the optimal combination and utilization of the resources but also the constraint of time sequence and causation of each task to obtain the final result. As a consequence, the cloud workflow scheduling problem is usually a NP-hard problem. The implications of cloud workflow scheduling research are as follows:

- It can promote the user's QoS request of gratification. It not only promotes the user's gratification of workflow execution cost, but also attracts the users to use cloud services, thus help to achieve maximum profit.
- It can improve the resource utilization of cloud services provided by cloud service provider. By taking the characteristic of workflow instance into account, the resource utilization involved in workflow scheduling will be significantly improved.
- It can promote the development and application of cloud computing and workflow technology, especially in the areas of biomedicine, chemistry, gene expression data analysis, astrophysics and the instance-intensive applications such as e-commerce, etc.

3   Typical Cloud Workflow Scheduling Algorithms

This section makes the typical cloud workflow scheduling algorithms with principle, merit and demerit sorting and analysis according to the scheduling difference of existing cloud workflows. We can divide the algorithms into three categories: single-objective optimization algorithms, multi-objective optimization algorithms, and heuristic algorithms for scheduling strategy and heuristic algorithms used.

3.1   Single-Objective Optimization Workflow Scheduling Algorithms

Cloud Workflow Scheduling Algorithm Oriented to Dynamic Price Changes

Min Zheng et al. [9] proposed a cloud workflow algorithm based on dynamic planning to solve the scheduling overhead optimization of cloud workflow in dynamic resource prices environment. Firstly, they define the model of workflow, resource and the target of task. Then, the cloud workflow tasks are divided into groups. Next, using the dynamic algorithm to dispatch each task and making the task links of workflow get better result. After grouping, the overall deadline will be allocated to each task group, and sort them topologically. At last, the dynamic algorithm is used to dispatch each task, and that the lowest overhead scheduling scheme in certain time is calculated.

Instance-Intensive Cost-Constrained Workflows Scheduling Algorithm in a Cloud
Mukute et al. [10] proposed an algorithm based on Job Shop to solve the issue of
dynamic scheduling in cloud computing with a special attention to the case of instance-intensive cost-constrained workflows. They first consider the classification and
combinatorial optimization of the concurrent tasks which need specified resources
with a certain number. Then they specify the priority for tasks and make user minimize the overall cost in the end.

Meeting Deadlines of Scientific Workflows with Tasks Replication
In order to address limitations of ignoring costs related to utilization of the infrastructure and he capacity of taking advantage of elastic infrastructures and other. Rodrigo
N. Calheiros and Rajkumar Buyya [17] proposed an algorithm, called EIPR, which
uses idle time of provisioned resources to replicate workflow tasks in order to miti-
gate effects of performance variation of resources so that the soft deadlines can be
met. The experiment result showed that the EIPR algorithm increases the chance of
deadlines being met and reduces the total execution time of workflow.

3.2   Multi-objective Optimization Workflow Scheduling Algorithms

Multi-objective Workflow Scheduling
Juan et al. proposed [11] a multi-objective workflow scheduling method called Multi-
Objective Heterogeneous Earliest Finish Time (MOHEFT) for multi-objective optimization problem in Amazon EC2 Cloud which offer heterogeneous types of
resources at different prices and with different performance. MOHEFT is a Pareto-
based list scheduling heuristic that provides the user with a set of tradeoff optimal
solutions from which the one that better suits the user requirements can be manually
selected. Finally, the experiments revealed that MOHEFT was able to meet the constraints imposed by current commercial Clouds in terms of the maximum amount of
instances.

Minimum Total Cost Under User-Designated Total Deadline Algorithm
Jing Yan et al. [8] proposed a scheduling algorithm, named Minimum Total Cost Under User-designated Total Deadline (MCUD), based on multiple instances. For the
workflow instances of the same type, after classification, MCUD algorithm distributes
the user-designated overall deadline into each task with a new distribution method. In
addition MCUD algorithm adjusts the sub-deadline of successive task dynamically
during the scheduling process. Instances of the same nature are given the sub-deadline
distribution results of some difference, which can avoid the fierce competition of
cheaper services and increase the efficiency of resource utilization.

Auto-Scaling to Minimize Cost and Meet Application Deadlines
Ming Mao [14] et al. proposed a new auto-scaling mechanism for deadline to avoid
the faults which the traditional "auto-scaling" mechanisms only support simple resource utilization indicators and do not specifically consider both user performance
requirements and budget concerns. What the auto-scaling mechanism they have

implemented is finishing all jobs by user specified deadlines in a cost-efficient way. The method based a monitor-control loop adapts to dynamic changes such as the workload bursting and delayed instance acquisitions. In experiments, it has shown great performance.

Scaling and Scheduling to Maximize Application Performance with Budget Constraints

Ming Mao [15] et al. proposed two auto-scaling mechanisms to solve the issue that how to maximize the return from the cloud investment. They have implemented two algorithms: the scheduling-first algorithm which distributes the application-wide budget to each individual job, determines the task scheduling plan first and then acquires the VMs, while the scaling-first algorithm determines the size and the cloud resources first and then schedules the workflow jobs on the acquired instances. The results show good tolerance to inaccurate parameters.

Compromise-Time-Cost Scheduling Algorithm

Liu Ke [6] et al. presented a novel compromised-time-cost scheduling algorithm which focus on the trade-off of time and cost throughout the scheduling process. They pay attention to the feature of cloud computing, the cost of execution and average execution time and make the trade-off dynamically under user preferences, to resolve the scheduling problem of instance-intensive cost-constrained workflows. The algorithm can be further decomposed into two sub-algorithms: CTC-MC (Compromised-Time-Cost algorithm Minimizing execution Cost) algorithm which minimizes the execution cost with user designated and CTC-MT (Compromised-Time-Cost algorithm Minimizing execution Time) algorithm which minimizes the execution time within user designated budget.

3.3   Heuristic Based Workflow Scheduling Algorithms

A Particle Swarm Optimization (PSO)-Based Heuristic for Scheduling Workflow Application in Cloud Computing Environments

In addition to optimizing execution time, the cost arising from data transfers between resources as well as execution costs must also be taken into account. Suraj Pandey et al. [12] proposed a particle swarm optimization (PSO) based scheduling heuristic for data intensive applications that take into account both computation cost and data transmission cost. They use the heuristic to minimize the total cost of execution of scientific application workflows on Cloud computing environments. They vary the communication cost between resources, the execution cost of compute resources and compare the results against "Best Resource Selection" (BRS) heuristic. The experiments show that PSO based task-resource mapping can achieve at least three times cost saving as compared to BRS based mapping.

Market-Oriented-Hierarchical Scheduling

Zhangjun Wu [7] et al. proposed a cloud workflow scheduling strategy based on intelligence algorithm and adaptation-aware of cloud services composition strategy which has been developed to scheduling the two-level cloud workflow tasks. The two-level schedulings are service level scheduling which selects suitable cloud service for task units called package-based scheduling and task level scheduling which allocates tasks to the virtual machine of data center dynamically. Service-level scheduling should satisfy the QoS constrain of each task and the dependency between tasks. The task-level scheduling research genetic algorithm, ant colony algorithm and particle swarm algorithm under QoS of each task and the total cost reduced. In brief, this strategy selects suitable cloud provider and books the service resource; allocates and optimizes tasks to virtual computing resource using intellectual algorithms in task-level.

Concurrent Level Based Workflow Scheduling Algorithm
Due to Deadline Bottom Level (DBL) hasn't considered the concurrence during the real executing process that cause much more shatter time. In order to solve such problem, Guangzhen Lu [13] et al. proposed a novel heuristic workflow scheduling algorithm CLWS, which it distributes task levels by their concurrence, and adopts the efficiency algorithm MDP to optimize the sequential tasks with time dependency. It not only can decrease the time pieces, but also can optimize the total executing cost. The experiments demonstrate that CLWS has better performance than DBL and Deadline Min-Cost.

Adaptive Workflow Scheduling
Mustafizur Rahman [16] et al. developed a hybrid heuristic that can effectively integrate most of the benefits of both heuristic and metaheuristic-based approaches to optimize execution cost and time as well as meet the user's requirements through an adaptive fashion. They proposed Adaptive Hybrid Heuristic scheduling algorithm, which is designed to first generate a task-to-service mapping with minimum execution cost using GA with user's budget and deadline as well as satisfying the service and data placement constraints specified by the user.

Table 1. The typical of clouding workflow algrithms

Scheduling Algorithm	Scheduling Method	Scheduling Parameters	Findings	Environment	Tools
Cloud workflow scheduling algorithm oriented to dynamic price changes	Batch /dependency mode	Execution cost, Deadline time	It decrease 5% cost compared to state space algorithm with considering the changing price	Cloud Environment	Java
Instance-intensive cost-constrained workflows scheduling algorithm	Batch /dependency mode	Resource Utilization, Total cost	The algorithm decrease the cost compared the built-in algorithm and has better performance	Cloud Environment	Cloud-Sim

Table 1. (*continued*)

Enhanced IC-PCP with Replication (EIPR) algorithm	Dependency mode	Deadline and total cost	Reduce execution time by 59% compared to the IC-PCP algorithm	Cloud Environment	Cloud-Sim
Multi-objective workflow scheduling	Batch /dependency mode	Execution cost, Total time	It saved 5% time compared to SPEA2* and HEFT with the cost decreased by half	Cloud Environment	Amazon EC2
Minimum Total Cost Under User-designated Total Deadline algorithm	Batch /dependency mode	Cost, Deadline time	It decrease 17% cost and 20% time compared to Deadline-MDP algorithm	Cloud Environment	Cloud-Sim
Auto-Scaling to Minimize Cost and Meet Application Deadlines	Dependency mode	Deadlines, cost and lag of instance	Save from 9.8% to 40.4% compared to other approaches	Cloud Environment	Other
Scaling and Scheduling to Maximize Application Performance with Budget Constraints	Dependency mode	Budget , workload and job turnaround time	Reduce the job turnaround time by 9.6%-45.2% and good tolerance	Cloud Environment	Cloud-Sim
Compromise-Cost-Time Algorithm	Batch mode	Cost, Time	Reduce the time and cost	Cloud Environment	Swin-DeW-C
A Particle Swarm Optization (PSO)-based Heuristic for Scheduling	Dependency mode	Computational and data transmission cost	It saved three times cost compared to BRS and has good distribution workload	Cloud Environment	Amazon EC2

Table 1. (*continued*)

Market-Oriented-Hierarchical Scheduling	Virtual clusters	Total cost, CPU time	Minimize the total execution cost	Cloud Environment	Cloud-Sim
Concurrent Level based Workflow Scheduling(CLWS)	Dependency mode	Cost with user designated	Decrease the time pieces and optimize the total executing cost.	Cloud Environment	Other
Adaptive Hybrid Heuristic scheduling algorithm	Dependency mode	Budget, deadline and execution cost	Identifie dynamic scheduling approaches	Cloud Environment	Other

As Table 1 shows, we make a comprehensive comparison with these algorithms, and make analysis based scheduling model, scheduling parameter, scheduling result, the tools and the environment they used. We can find that all algorithms used above are cloud-based environment. Most of algorithms are batch-based and dependency-based, and the simulation based CloudSim or other simulators. The batch-based is clustering some relatively separate instances to dispatch; and the dependency-based is that the single instance composed of multi-activity instances; and what the dispatch of Virtual clusters is that using integrated tasks and virtual machines to define the local task and virtual machine list which are the input of scheduling algorithm. Most of algorithms focus on the execution cost and time which are the two hot research areas. In addition, all the scheduling results of algorithms have better performance than the non-optimized algorithms.

4   Typical Tools for Cloud Workflow Scheduling Research

4.1   CloudSim[1]

Cloud computing can satisfy the different service requests with different configuration, deployment condition and service resources of various user at different time point. With the influence of multidimensional factors, it is unreality to test with different parameters in actual cloud computing center. So CloudSim, WorkflowSim and so on have been used for simulating with cloud workflow scheduling.

CloudSim is a toolkit (library) for simulation of cloud computing scenarios. It provides basic classes for describing data centers, virtual machines, applications, users, computational resources, and policies for management of diverse parts of the system (e.g., scheduling and provisioning) [18].

---

[1] http://www.cloudbus.org/cloudsim

The main features of CloudSim are following:

1. Support for modeling and simulation of large scale Cloud computing data centers;
2. A self-contained platform for modeling Clouds, service brokers, provisioning, and allocation polices;
3. Support for simulation of network connections among the simulated system elements;
4. Facility for simulation of federated Cloud environment that inter-networks resources form both private and public domains.

Above these, the researchers can evaluate the hypothesis prior to a real deployment in an environment with CloudSim, where one can reproduce tests, while they can also test the new developmental methodologies and policies in cloud computing environment. CloudSim can bring us some benefits: (I) to test the performance of their provisioning and service delivery policies in a repeatable and controllable environment free of cost; and (II) to tune the performance bottlenecks before real-world deployment on commercial Clouds.

4.2   WorkflowSim[2]

WorkflowSim extends the CloudSim simulation toolkit by introducing the support of workflow preparation and execution with an implementation of a stack of workflow parser, workflow engine and job scheduler. It supports a multi-layered model of failures and delays occurring in the various levels of the workflow management systems. The architecture of WorkflowSim is shown in Figure 1.

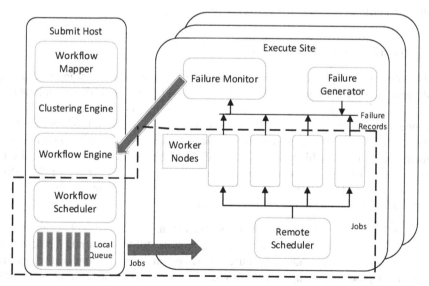

Fig. 1. WorkflowSim Overview. The area surrounded by dotted lines is supported by CloudSim.

---

[2] http://www.workflowsim.org

As it shows, the submit host consists of Workflow Mapper which maps abstract workflows to concrete workflows that are dependent on execution sites, Clustering Engine which merges small tasks into a large job such that the scheduling overhead is reduced, and Workflow Engine which handles the data dependencies and local scheduler and that only releases free tasks to Clustering Engine. The Execution Site consists of Remote Scheduler which is used to match jobs to a worker node based on the criteria selected by users, Worker Nodes, Failure Generator which is introduced to inject task/job failures at each execution site during the simulation and Failure Monitor which collects failure records to return these records to Clustering Engine to adjust the scheduling strategies dynamically [19].

In actual operation process, as the workflow is so numerous, even contains tens of thousands of tasks, while we usually have only dozens of computing nodes, task clustering needed to use for polymerizing similar tasks at this moment, and form clustered job accordingly, which generally called job. Each job include several tasks, and integrally submit to operating environment, in this way can save a lot of submission delay, and open and execute the clustered job separately when a certain computing node is available.

WorkflowSim is used for validating Graph algorithm, distributed computing, workflow scheduling, resource provisioning and so on. In addition, WorkflowSim is an open source workflow simulator that has been hosted on GitHub[3]. Compared to CloudSim and other workflow simulators, WorkflowSim provides support of task clustering that merges tasks into a cluster job and dynamic scheduling algorithm that jobs matched to a worker node whenever a worker node become idle. A series of popular workflow scheduling algorithm (e.g., HEFT, Min-Min, and Max-Min) and task clustering algorithms have been implemented in WorkflowSim. Users can specify different criteria to optimize the overall performance.

4.3   SwinDeW-C and SwinFlow-Cloud

Instance-intensive application is one ubiquitous workflow application in real life, but traditional workflow systems cannot give an enough support to these applications. Therefore, the group led by Yun Yang professor has proposed the concepts of instance-intensive workflow, and focused on research of the design of system architecture, scheduling algorithms. The cloud workflow systems have gained rapid development, the typical of which are SwinDeW-C based on SwinDeW-G from Swinburne University of Technology, Cloud based on Hadoop from University of Waterloo, Cloudbus Engine based on Gridbus from University of Melbourne. The design of cloud workflow system architecture is following:

The workflow system architecture has improved from centralized architecture to decentralized architecture. But centralized architecture is still the most popular paradigm in today's workflow community because it is simple and easy to rapidly implement a prototype or product to support workflows. The client-server model also is a typical

---

[3] https://github.com/WorkflowSim/WorkflowSim-1.0

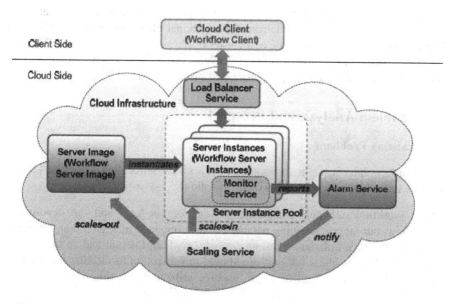

Fig. 2. Cloud workflow system architecture of supporting instance-intensive application

centralized architecture, such as IBM FileNet, TIBCO iProcess Suite and so on. In addition, although Amazon launched the Simple Workflw (SWF) which can set up the extensible and elastic workflow applications, and can coordinate each step in application, it cannot effectively support the high throughput workflow. While there are a huge amount of user service requests needed to handle at one time in instance-intensive workflow, what the most important is how to maximize the system throughput.

Above these faults in instance-intensive workflow, Swinburne Decentralized Workflow for Cloud which evolved from a series of SwinDeW projects has been set up by the group of Yun Yang. It is a cloud workflow prototype system built on Swin-Cloud, and contains four basic layers: Application Layer (User application), Platform Layer (cloud services of middleware, deploy user application), Uniform Resources Layer (abstract/encapsulate the virtual resources), and Physical Layer (hardware resources) [20].

The researchers can describe the cloud workflow application as cloud workflow description which include definition, flowage structure and QoS constraint by modeling tool of SwinDew-C. Then they can make a static verification with the flowage structure and QoS constraint. Next, previous description will be submitted the coordinating nodes. In the stage of workflow instantiation, coordinating nodes allocate the description to suitable nodes. At last, that is workflow execution, tasks will be scheduled on VMs of SwinDew-C to execute. SwinDeW-C also support outside business IaaS, such as offered by Amazon, Google, and Microsoft.

Soon after, Dahai Cao et al. [21] proposed a novel client-cloud architecture for scalable workflow system which takes advantages of cloud computing to support instance-intensive workflow and built the SwinFlow-Cloud prototype system. Client-cloud means that the client communicates with an elastic pool of workflow server instances on the cloud side, which is different from the traditional client-server model where the client communicates with one static or a cluster of physical workflow servers. The high throughput, elastic scalability and cost-effectiveness have been taken account into the system, so it can achieve a dynamic, elastic, and sustainable scalability.

5   Problem Analysis and Prospect

5.1   Existing Problems

The researchers have made great progress in Workflow Scheduling Algorithms so far. But there are also some problems in them, as follows:

1. Most workflow scheduling algorithms focus on the cost and the deadline of workflow, but other scheduling parameters have obtained little attention, for example, like resource utilization, resource reliability, fault-tolerant and so on. The resource in cloud is huge, not only we should pay attention to meeting the deadline but also the improvement of singe resource utilization. At this time, we should solve the problem when the execution happens faults, too.
2. Lack of the workflow task model in cloud. Always, it is more practicability when workflow scheduling algorithms have been made verification. But in the current cloud environment, most researchers just use simple mathematical model or directed acyclic graph because of lacking task log. Most task models are not made according to the specific operational tasks in cloud, the experimental results are least persuasion, so the problem of making appropriate model in cloud needs to be resolved urgently.
3. Most workflow scheduling algorithms have been implemented in cloud simulators, besides the scientific workflow. We must apply workflow scheduling algorithms in real-life environment so that can solve more real practical problem.

5.2   Prospect

1. The reliability should been considered in workflow scheduling algorithms, the robustness can have a significant impact on experiment. Taking the reliability and robustness into account can close to real situation.
2. Duplication based on workflow scheduling algorithm. The parts of tasks can be automatically duplicated to the free computing nodes which have some savings.
3. To be combined with the practical application. Today, most workflow scheduling are used in simulation environment, while it still has some deficiencies compared with real environment.

6   Conclusion

The optimization of cloud workflow scheduling can make full use of various cloud services, which will greatly promote the execution of a workflow. Workflow scheduling is the most important problem in the execution of workflow management in cloud. In this paper, we research several typical cloud computing workflow scheduling algorithms and make a detailed analysis and comparison for them. Meanwhile, we also give a detail about cloud computing tools, like CLoudSim, WorkflowSim and other cloud simulation tools. CloudSim can facilitate the research of the cloud computing simulation and make it easy for researchers to set up their experimental platform; while WorkflowSim and other systems can help researchers process the workflow scheduling optimization according to their own requirements and parameters. At last, we point out the existing problems of workflow scheduling algorithms and put forward some opinions and the direction of improvement., In conclusion, the significant findings of workflow scheduling algorithms in the cloud have been obtained but more progress is still need.

Acknowledgment. This paper was supported by Nature Science Fund of China, under grant number 61272063, 61402167, 61202111, 61402168, the Planned Science and Technology Project of Hunan Province under grant number 13FJ4048, 2014GK3004, and Scientific Research Fund of Hunan Provincial Education Department under grant number 13C160.

References

1. Chai, X., Cao, J.: Cloud Computing Oriented Workflow Technology. Journal of Chinese Computer Systems 33(1), 90–95 (2012)
2. Fan, Y.: Fundamentals of Workflow Management Technology. TUP, Beijing (2001)
3. Yao, H., Tian, S.: Cloud Computing. Electronics Industry Publisher (2013)
4. Buyya, R., Broberg, J., Goscinski, A.: Cloud Computing: Principles and Paradigms. John Wiley & Sons (2010)
5. Bala, A., Chana, I.: A survey of various workflow scheduling algorithms in cloud environment. In: Proc. of the 2nd National Conference on Information and Communication Technology, pp. 26–30 (2011)
6. Liu, K., Yang, Y., Chen, J., et al.: A Compromised-Cost Scheduling Algorithm in Swin-DeW-C for Instance-intensive Cost-Constrained Workflows on Cloud Computing Platform. International Journal of High Performance Computing Applications 24(4), 445–456 (2010)
7. Wu, Z., Liu, X., Ni, Z., Yuan, D., Yang, Y.: A market-oriented hierarchical scheduling strategy in cloud workflow systems. The Journal of Supercomputing 63(1), 256–293 (2013)
8. Yan, J., Wu, G.: Scheduling Algorithm for Instance-Intensive Cloud workflow. Journal of Computer Applications 30(243), 2864–2866 (2010)
9. Zheng, M., Cao, J., Yao, Y.: Cloud Workflow Scheduling Algorithm Oriented to Dynamic Pric Changes. Computer Integrated Manufacturing Systems 19(8), 1849–1858 (2013)
10. Mukute, S., Hapanyengwi, G., Mapako, B., et al.: Scheduling in Instance-Intensive Cost-Constrained Workflows in a Cloud. International Journal of Scientific & Engineering Research 4, 755–760 (2013)
11. Durillo, J.J., Prodan, R.: Multi-objective workflow scheduling in Amazon EC2. Cluster Computing 17(2), 169–189 (2014)

12. Pandey, S., Wu, L., Guru, S.M., Buyya, R.: A particle swarm optimization-based heuristic for scheduling workflow applications in cloud computing environments. In: Proc. of the 24th IEEE International Conference on Advanced Information Networking and Applications (AINA), pp. 400–407 (2010)
13. Lu, G., Tan, W., Sun, Y., Zhang, Z., Tang, A.: QoS Constraint Based Workflow Scheduling for Cloud Computing Services. Journal of Software 9(4), 926–930 (2014)
14. Mao, M., Humphrey, M.: Auto-scaling to minimize cost and meet application deadlines in cloud workflows. In: Proc. of 2011 International Conference for High Performance Computing, Networking, Storage and Analysis, p. 49. ACM (2011)
15. Mao, M., Humphrey, M.: Scaling and Scheduling to Maximize Application Performance within Budget Constraints in Cloud Workflows. In: Proc. of the 27th IEEE International Parallel & Distributed Processing Symposium (IPDPS 2013), pp. 67–78 (2013)
16. Rahman, M., Hassan, M.R., Ranjan, R., Buyya, R.: Adaptive workflow scheduling for dynamic grid and cloud computing environment. Concurrency and Computation: Practice and Experience 25(13), 1816–1842 (2013)
17. Calheiros, R.N., Buyya, R.: Meeting Deadlines of Scientific Workflows in Public Clouds with Tasks Replication. IEEE Transactions on Parallel and Distributed Systems 25(7), 1787–1796 (2013)
18. Buyya, R., Ranjan, R., Calheiros, R.N.: Modeling and simulation of scalable Cloud computing environments and the CloudSim toolkit: Challenges and opportunities. In: Proc. of the IEEE International Conference on High Performance Computing & Simulation (HPCS 2009), pp. 1–11 (2009)
19. Chen, W., Deelman, E.: Workflowsim: A toolkit for simulating scientific workflows in distributed environments. In: Proc. of the 8th IEEE International Conference on E-Science, pp. 1–8 (2012)
20. Liu, X., Yuan, D., Zhang, G., et al.: SwinDeW-C: a peer-to-peer based cloud workflow system. In: Handbook of Cloud Computing, pp. 309–332. Springer US (2010)
21. Cao, D., Liu, X., Yang, Y.: Novel Client-Cloud Architecture for Scalable Instance-Intensive Workflow Systems. In: Lin, X., Manolopoulos, Y., Srivastava, D., Huang, G. (eds.) WISE 2013, Part II. LNCS, vol. 8181, pp. 270–284. Springer, Heidelberg (2013)

Q-learning Algorithm for Task Allocation Based on Social Relation

Xingmei Liu, Jian Chen, Yu Ji, and Yang Yu

School of Information Science and Technology
Sun Yat-Sen University
Guangzhou, Guangdong, P.R.China

Abstract. Social relation has a great impact on task allocation of a workflow management system. Most methods only focus on analyzing the effect of the handover relation. However, a workflow is a team process since many resources work on various tasks together to complete an instance. So the influence of the previous resources (called SR) should be considered during dynamic task allocation. This paper proposes a method to compute the social relation between two resources. Then we present a model to capture the influence of the previous resources on the candidate resources and implement a Q-learning algorithm for dynamic task allocation based on flow time perspective. Comparison experiments show that the algorithm with SR has almost 53% improvement of a real data set and 40% improvement of a simulation data set in flow time perspective. There is a higher throughput than the algorithm without SR. Experiment results confirm the existence of such relationship and prove that it is necessary to consider the influence of all previous resources during dynamic task allocation.

Keywords: task allocation, social relation, markov decision process, Q-learning.

1   Introduction

Task allocation is an important issue in Business Process Management. The workflow engine should allocate tasks to appropriate resources in order to improve the performance of business process. Resources can be divided into human resources and non-human resources in workflow management system [1]. And there are many factors influencing the human resources behavior. For example, the workload of the human will affect the humans ability, namely Yerkes-Dodson Law of Arousal, which shows that a worker will take less time to execute an task if he/she is under some work pressure [2]. However, if the pressure is too high, the worker's performance may degrade. And the social relation between two resources also has influence on work efficiency. However, most papers only focus on the handover relation which means the candidate resources who will perform successive task will be affected by the resource who performed the precursor task [3]. In reality, many people are involved in a task at the same time, just like a

J. Cao et al. (Eds.): PAS 2014, CCIS 495, pp. 49–58, 2015.
© Springer-Verlag Berlin Heidelberg 2015

work team completing a process together. As a result, all the previous resources
may affect the candidate resources of the successive task. This is because the
candidate resources may need to refer back to the resources of the previous tasks.

There were many algorithms for task allocation. Such as the shortest work
list allocation, the shortest processing time allocation and the shortest complete
time allocation [4]. All these algorithms have some disadvantages such as load
imbalance [4]. Q-learning is a more effective algorithm for task allocation, the
reasons are as follow: first, task allocation is an interactive problem which can
be modeled as Markov Decision Processes (MDPs), and Q-learning is a reinforcement learning algorithm that can be used to solve the MDPs problems;
second, Q-learning algorithm can choose the optimal action to achieve its goals
through learning without the knowledge of state's transfer function [5]; third,
the Q-learning algorithm can make resource's load balance.

In this paper, a method to compute the social relation between two resources
and a model to capture the influence of the previous resources when doing task
allocation are presented. The task allocation problem is modeled as a MDPs
problem, which is solved by Q-learning algorithm. A real world data set and a
simulated data set are used in the experiment. Using these data sets can prove
the idea better.

The paper is organized as follow: Section 2 introduces the related work about
task allocation and reinforcement learning algorithm; Section 3 gives concepts
and definitions proposed in this paper; Section 4 describes the MDPs model
of task allocation; Section 5 gives details of the Q-learning algorithm for task
allocation; Experiment and results are described in Section 6; Conclusions are
made in Section 7.

2   Related Work

2.1   Task Allocation

Task allocation in business process aims to choose the appropriate resources to
do certain tasks. Resource's behavior influences the performance of the workflow
management system, and many other factors affect the resources behavior at the
same time. Joyce Nakatumba and WilM.P.van der Aalst et al. used process mining to explore the effect of workload on service time of every resource which is
known as "Yerkes-Dodson Law of Arousal" [6]. They also presented an approach
based on regression analysis to quantify the relationship between workload and
processing speed. In [7], the author proposed a novel resource model of resources'
community, which was also used to accelerate the collaboration between various
resources. But the concept of teamwork wasn't used for dynamic task allocation.
The interest of resource on the task would be considered in [8], it is difficult to
measure this index exactly in reality. Yi Liu et al. presented a strategy for task
allocation which supported load-balancing of resources and considered experiential value [9]. However, it is difficult to measure the experiential value precisely
in reality. Jiaxing Xu et al. presented social context which only considered the
handover relation [3].

2.2   Reinforcement Learning Algorithm

The reinforcement learning is an algorithm which agent makes decision based on the feedback through the interacting with the current environment state. The reinforcement leaning algorithm is divided into two types according to the optimizing index of MDPs [10]. One is the discounted return index reinforcement learning, the other is the average reward reinforcement learning. $TD(\lambda)$, Sarsa learning and Q-learning is the first type. R learning and H learning is the second type. The reinforcement learning is widely used to solve problems in different fields. For example, R-learning was used to study parallel machines scheduling problems which aimed to minimize the flow time of jobs [11]. It is the average reward reinforcement learning so that it is not suitable to solve the workflow problems. Mehmet Emin Aydin et al. tried to used Q-learning to solve the job-shop scheduling problem [12]. Zhengxing Huang et al. used Q-learning to address work distribution problems of business process management [13][14]. These papers show that Q-learning has the ability to solve the workflow problems modeled by MDPs.

3   Concepts and Definitions

3.1   Social Relation between Two Resources

Before computing the influence of the previous resources on the current candidate resources, the social relation factor between each tow resources should be calculated first. The social relation between r_2 and r_1 can be defined as follow:

$$SR_{r_2,r_1} = \frac{t_{r_2,r_1} - t}{t} \tag{1}$$

Here t_{r_2,r_1} is the processing time of the resource r_2 when collaborated with r_1, and t is average processing time of the resource r_2 related to a certain task.

Obviously, if r_1 and r_2 collaborates well, SR_{r_2,r_1} will be a negative number. It means that it will cost shorter time when r_2 collaborate with r_1. If SR_{r_2,r_1} is a positive number, the collaborated resources fail to promote each other.

3.2   The Influence of the Previous Resources

According to formula (1), the processing time t_{r_3,r_2} of the resource r_3 when collaborated with r_2 or r_1 is

$$t_{r_3,r_2} = (1 + SR_{r_3,r_2}) * t$$

$$t_{r_3,r_1} = (1 + SR_{r_3,r_1}) * t$$

So the processing time t_{r_3,r_2,r_1} of the resources r_3 when collaborated with r_2 and r_1 is

$$t_{r_3,r_2,r_1} = \frac{t_{r_3,r_2} + t_{r_3,r_1}}{2} = (1 + \frac{SR_{r_3,r_2} + SR_{r_3,r_1}}{2}) * t$$

Then, the formula to compute the influence of the previous resources on the current resources in processing time is defined as follow:

$$t_{r_n,r_{n-1},r_{n-2},r_{n-3},...r_2,r_1} = (1 + \frac{1}{n-1} \sum_{i=1}^{n-1} SR_{r_n,r_i}) * t \tag{2}$$

Where, $t_{r_n,r_{n-1},r_{n-2},r_{n-3},...r_2,r_1}$ means the processing time of r_n when its previous resources are $r_1, r_2, r_3...r_{n-1}$ and t is the average processing time of r_n no matter who performs the previous tasks.

4   The Problem Model

The task allocation problem can be modeled as MDPs. The traditional MDPs can be simply described as follow: the agent can choose an action from the set of actions; then the environment changed and the agent goes into another state after executing that action, and it receives the action's immediate payoff [14]. A MDPs is a tuple $< S, A, P, R >$, where :

- S is a set of possible states of the environment;
- A is a set of possible actions of the system;
- P is a state transfer function, which input $S \times A$, then output a real number, namely $\delta(s, a(s)) \rightarrow S$, where $s \in S$, $a(s) \in A$, $a(s)$ means the set of actions in state s;
- R is a immediate payoff function, which input $S \times A$, then output a real number, namely $\delta(s, a(s)) \rightarrow S$, where $s \in S$, $a(s) \in A$, $a(s)$ means the set of actions in state s.

In the following part, the detail of the MDPs for the task allocation problem will be described.

4.1   State Space

Let S be a set of states, $S \in T \times WL$. Where:

- let T be a finite set of tasks;
- let WL be a set of the workload of all resources.

For example, considering a particular state $s_\tau = (t, wl_\tau)$, where:

- $t \in T$, is a task in the workflow model;
- τ is the moment of the making decision when an enabled work item should be allocated;
- $wl \in WL$, $wl \in \{r.wl | r \in R\}$, which is one possible condition of all candidate resources work list.

4.2   Action State

Let A be a set of actions, A=R, where, R is a set of the resources in the workflow model. Let $a(s) = candidates(s.t)$ be a set of the optional actions in the state s, where $s.t$ means the task t is allocated in state s.

4.3   Reward Function

In this paper, the objective is minimizing the flow time of the business process cases. So the reward function should be defined as:

$$r = \begin{cases} \frac{1}{\sigma.fl}, & (t \text{ is } None) \\ 0, & (else) \end{cases} \tag{3}$$

Where, t is a task will be allocated, σ is the current determinative case, $\sigma.fl$ is the flow time of the case. The shorter flow time $\sigma.fl$ takes, the higher immediate payoff r returns. The agent will receive the reward when the last work item is completed, otherwise the reward is zero.

5   Q-learning Algorithm for MDPs

Q-learning is a more suitable algorithm to solve the problem modeled by MDPs [15]. In this section, the detail of the proposed Q-learning algorithm will be described. In order to verify the influence of the previous resources on the candidate resources, the Q-learning algorithm without SR is used as the basic experiment. The basic experiment will be described in the first part, and the second part will introduce the Q-learning algorithm with SR.

5.1   The Q-learning Algorithm without SR

In order to realize the Q-learning algorithm, the evaluation function $Q(s,a)$ and the estimation function $\hat{Q}(s,a)$ was defined [15]. According to MDPs, the evaluation function $Q(s,a)$ can be written as:

$$Q(s,a) \equiv (r(s,a) + \gamma max_{a'} Q(\delta(s,a), a') \tag{4}$$

We can use $\hat{Q}$ to evaluate the Q function, then the agent can update $\hat{Q}(s,a)$ according to the following rules:

$$\hat{Q}(s,a) \leftarrow r + \gamma max_{a'} \hat{Q}(s', a') \tag{5}$$

For the situation of non deterministic reward and action, formula (5) will be replaced by the following formula:

$$\hat{Q}_n(s,a) \leftarrow (1 - \alpha_n)\hat{Q}_{n-1}(s,a) + \alpha_n[r + \gamma max_{a'}\hat{Q}_{n-1}(s', a')] \tag{6}$$

Where,

$$\alpha_n = \frac{1}{1 + visits_n(s,a)}$$

$visits_n(s, a)$ is the accessed total number of the state-action pair (s,a) within n loops.

And in order to facilitate the iterative approximation of $Q(s, a)$, one state-action pair (s,a) is mapped to a Q value. In this paper, there is:

$$(s, a) = ((t, wl), a) = (t, wl, a) \subseteq T \times Wl \times R$$

Where, T and R are finite sets. Let $t \in T$ is the task will be allocated. The workload of one resource $r \in candidates(t)$ is defined as $wl(r)$:

$$wl(r) = \begin{cases} FREE, & (|r.wl| = 0) \\ LOW, & (|r.wl| \leq avg\_wl(t)) \\ HIGH, & (|r.wl| > avg\_wl(t)) \end{cases} \tag{7}$$

Here, the function $avg\_wl(t)$ is the average length of all candidate resources' work list for the task t. For example, if there are no enabled work items that are allocated to the resource r, $wl(r) = FREE$, and if the work list's length of the resource r is less (higher) than the $avg\_wl(t)$, $wl(r) = LOW(HIGH)$.

Intuitively, the estimation function $\hat{Q}(s, a)$ can be mapped to a big table:

$$\hat{Q} = Q\_Table(t, r, wl(r))$$

For instance, $Q\_Table(t1, r1, FREE)$ is a value achieved from formula (6) when task $t1$ is allocated to resource $r1$ and its workload is $FREE$.

Table1 shows the main steps of Q-learning algorithm for task allocation without SR as follow:

Table 1. Q-learning Algorithm without SR

---

1 For each s and a, the Q_Table value is initialized as 0.
2 Get the current state s
3 Repeat until the system stop:
4   Choose the resource r_{pick} according to the value of $\hat{Q}(s, a)$, $a \leftarrow r_{pick}$, and then allocate the task t to r_{pick}
5   Allocate processing time for the task
6   Save (s, a) according to the corresponding case
7   A new enabled item is came or a work item is completed.
8   Get a new state s'
9   Read (s, a) according to the new case σ'
10   Receive the reward r
11   Update the Q_Table value according to the following formula:
12    $\hat{Q}_n(s, a) \leftarrow (1 - \alpha_n)\hat{Q}_{n-1}(s, a) + \alpha_n[r + \gamma max_{a'}\hat{Q}_{n-1}(s', a')]$
13    $s \leftarrow s', \sigma \leftarrow \sigma'$

5.2   The Q-learning Algorithm with SR

The main steps of Q-learning algorithm with SR are the same as the Q-learning algorithm without SR. It just needs to change the state space defined in section 4 as following:

Let $S_{SR} \in T \times R \times WL$ be a set of states, where:

- let T be a finite set of tasks;
- let R be a finite set of previous resources;
- let WL be a set of the workload of all resources.

For example, considering a particular state $s_\tau = (t2, r_{exs}, wl_\tau) \in S_{SR}$, which means the agent is allocating $t2$ now and r_{exs} is the previous resources of the completed work items in the same case. Because of the changed state space, the $\hat{Q}_n(s, a)$ function should be changed as:

$$\hat{Q}(s, a) = Q\_Table(t, r_{exs}, r, wl(r))$$

6   Experiment

The experiment of this paper is to analyze the performance of task allocation with SR under the assumption that the previous resources have influence on the candidate resources. So in this section, the performance of the one with SR will be compared with Q-learning without SR. The analysis of the result from the average Flow time and Throughput perspectives is also shown here.

6.1   Experiment Setting

The even log of a real-life process of BPI Challenge 2012[i] [1] which taken from a Dutch financial institute will be used for simulation. About 6078 cases, 5 activities and 55 resources are acquired from the real log. In Fig.1, the process model is expressed in terms of a workflow net [16]. The process may start with the $W\_Afhandelenleads$ with probability 0.46 or start with $W\_Completerenaanvraag$ with probability 0.54.

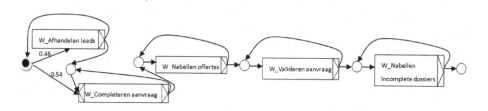

Fig. 1. A Real-life Financial Process

[1] http://www.win.tue.nl/bpi/2012/challenge

Because every different task has different probability of self-loop in reality, so self-loop probability of every task is set as 0.2 for the convenience of calculation. If discounted factor γ is large, the return has greater effect on Q value than the immediate payoff [15]. γ will be set as 0.9 in this paper. A detailed description of data sets is described in the follow:

(1) A data set from real log

The resource's average processing time for each task can be obtained from the real log. And the social relation between two resources will be computed according to the real log. Then calculate each resource's processing time when it is affected by other resources.

(2) A simulated data set

Because some resources' processing time is too big compare to other resources' processing time for the same task, which can be considered as noise of the data set. So the resources average processing time for each task will be simulated to almost the same size for the experiment.

6.2   Results and Analysis

Fig.2 shows the results of the Q-learning algorithm with and without on flow time perspective. X-axis is number of execution times, and Y-axis is the average flow time. Because the SR has less effect in early iterations, so in the first 100 executions, the resources are randomly chosen. And in the last 100 executions, the resources with highest Q value will be chosen.

The result shows that in the last 100 executions is better than the first 100 executions no matter in the experiment with SR or not. This verifies the theory which Q-learning algorithm can choose an optimal route for task allocation.

The resources' processing time for the same task of the real data set has a huge difference. The randomly process may choose the resource with the longest processing time in one execution and choose the resource with the shortest processing time in another execution. So there are obvious fluctuations in the result of the first 100 executions in Fig.2(a). In Fig.2(b), the average flow time of algorithm with and without SR in the first 100 executions is similar, which shows that the result of random scheduling is the same no matter considering SR or not. And the average flow time of the algorithm with SR is lower than the one without SR in the last 100 executions, which means taking social relation into consideration for task allocation will improve works efficiency.

Fig.3(a) shows the average flow time of 100 cases in one execution. The results with SR have an improvement of almost 53% of the real data set. The results minimized to 50.79 minutes with SR and 84.85 minutes without SR of the simulated data set. It has an improvement of about 40% when considering SR in the scheduling time. The real data set has a bigger improvement because its resources processing time has a bigger fluctuation. In other words, taking social relation into consideration for task allocation is efficiency.

Fig.3(b) shows the results of the Q-learning algorithm with and without SR on throughput perspective. Here the throughput is the number of completed cases in one hour. The throughput of the Q-learning algorithm without SR is

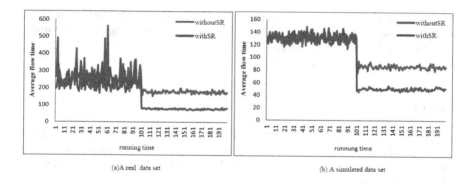

(a)A real data set   (b) A simulated data set

Fig. 2. The Average Flow Time of 200 Executions

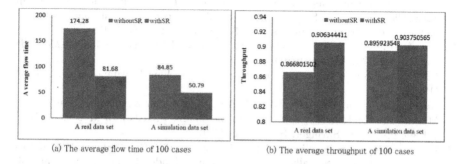

(a) The average flow time of 100 cases   (b) The average throughput of 100 cases

Fig. 3. The Average Flow Time and Throughput of 100 Cases

about 0.8, and the result with SR is about 0.9. The throughput with SR is a little better. The result means workflow management system can finish more cases in unit time if considering previous resources influence on candidate resources.

7 Conclusions

In this paper, we introduce a method to capture the social relation between two resources, and then compute the influence of the previous resources on the candidate resources according to the social relation. The experiment was conducted with a real life log and a simulated data set. The results show that considering the social relation for task allocation will improve the performance of the workflow management system. And the Q-learning algorithm is proved to be suitable for task allocation. So it is necessary to consider the social relation for task allocation. However, the experiment considers little about workload. So the resources workload should be defined more accurate in the future work.

Acknowledgment. This work is Supported by the National Natural Science Foundation of China under Grant No.60873162; the Natural Science Foundation of Guangdong Province under Grant No.S2012010009634; the Research Foundation of Science and Technology Major Project in Guangdong Province under Grant No.2012A010800012 ; the Research Foundation of Science and Technology Plan Project in Guangzhou City under Grant No.12A12051586 .

References

1. Russell, N., van der Aalst, W.M.P., ter Hofstede, A.H.M., Edmond, D.: Workflow Resource Patterns: Identification, Representation and Tool Support. In: Pastor, Ó., Falcão e Cunha, J. (eds.) CAiSE 2005. LNCS, vol. 3520, pp. 216–232. Springer, Heidelberg (2005)
2. Justin, G.H., Wickens, C.D.: Engineering Psychology and Human Performance (1999)
3. Jiaxing, X., Zhengguang, H., Yang, Y., Maolin, P.: A Performance Analysis on Task Allocation Using Social Context. In: 2012 Second International Conference on Cloud and Green Computing (CGC), pp. 637–644. IEEE (2012)
4. van der Aalst, W.M.P., van Hee, K.: Workflow Management: Models, Methods, and Systems. MIT Press (2002)
5. Christopher, J.C.H.W., Peter, D.: Q-learning. Machine Learning 8(3-4), 279–292 (1992)
6. Nakatumba, J., van der Aalst, W.M.P.: Analyzing Resource Behavior Using Process Mining. In: Rinderle-Ma, S., Sadiq, S., Leymann, F. (eds.) BPM 2009. LNBIP, vol. 43, pp. 69–80. Springer, Heidelberg (2010)
7. Liu, R., Agarwal, S., Sindhgatta, R.R., Lee, J.: Accelerating Collaboration in Task Assignment Using a Socially Enhanced Resource Model. In: Daniel, F., Wang, J., Weber, B. (eds.) BPM 2013. LNCS, vol. 8094, pp. 251–258. Springer, Heidelberg (2013)
8. Chuanbo, C., Weiwei, Z.: Strategy for a Task Assignment of Workflow System. Journal of Huazhong University of Science and Technology (Nature Science Edition) 33(6), 20–22 (2005)
9. Yi, L., Kan, Z.: Strategy for Workflow Task Assignment Based on Load Balance and Experiential Value. Computer Engineering 35(21), 57–59 (2009)
10. Yang, G., Ru Yi, Z., Hao, W., Zhixin, C.: Study on an Average Reward Reinforcement Learning Algorithm. Chinese Journal of Computers 30 (2007)
11. Zhicong, Z., Li, Z., Xiaohua, W.: Parallel Machines Scheduling with Reinforcement Learning. Computer Integrated Manufacturing Systems 13 (2007)
12. Emin, A.M., Öztemel, E.: Dynamic Job-shop Scheduling Using Reinforcement Learning Agents. Robotics and Autonomous Systems 33(2), 169–178 (2000)
13. Zhengxing, H., van der Aalst, W.M.P., Xudong, L., Huilong, D.: An Adaptive Work Distribution Mechanism Based on Reinforcement Learning. Expert Systems with Applications 37(12), 7533–7541 (2010)
14. Zhengxing, H., van der Aalst, W.M.P., Xudong, L., Huilong, D.: Reinforcement Learning Based Resource Allocation in Business Process Management. Data & Knowledge Engineering 70(1), 127–145 (2011)
15. Tom, M.M.: Mechine Learning. China Machine Press (2003)
16. van der Aalst, W.M.P.: The Application of Petri Nets to Workflow Management. Journal of Circuits, Systems, and Computers 8(01), 21–66 (1998)

Temporal Verification for Scientific Cloud Workflows: State-of-the-Art and Research Challenges

Qiudan Wang[1], Xiao Liu[1], Zhou Zhao[1], and Futian Wang[2]

[1] Shanghai Key Laboratory of Trustworthy Computing, East China Normal University, China
[2] School of Computer Science and Technology, Anhui University, China
qiudan.wang@outlook.com, xliu@sei.ecnu.edu.cn,
zzhao901@gmail.com, wft@ahu.edu.cn

Abstract. Cloud computing is establishing itself as the latest computing paradigm in recent years. As doing science in the cloud is becoming a reality, scientists are now able to access public cloud centers and employ high-performance computing resources to run scientific applications. However, due to the dynamic nature of the cloud environment, the usability of scientific cloud workflow systems can be significantly deteriorated if without effective service quality assurance strategies. Specifically, workflow temporal verification as the major approach for workflow temporal QoS (Quality of Service) assurance plays a critical role in the on-time completion of large-scale scientific workflows. Great efforts have been dedicated to the area of workflow temporal verification in recent years and it is high time that we should define the key research issues for scientific cloud workflows in order to keep our research on the right track. In this paper, we systematically investigate this problem and present four key research issues based on the introduction of a generic temporal verification framework. Meanwhile, state-of-the-art solutions for each research issue and open challenges are also presented. Finally, SwinDeW-V, an ongoing research project on temporal verification as part of our SwinDeW-C cloud workflow system, is also demonstrated.

Keywords: Scientific Workflow, Workflow Temporal Verification, Cloud Computing, Quality of Service.

1 Introduction

Many complex e-science applications such as climate modeling, earthquake modeling, weather forecast, Astrophysics and high energy physics require high-performance computing infrastructures [15]. In addition, since scientific applications are often collaborative processes among groups of scientists and require geographically distributed scientific equipment and data resources, modern scientific applications can normally be carried out in the form of scientific workflows [55]. A survey of scientific workflow systems can be found at [54]. The last decade has seen a significant development of distributed workflow systems with the grid computing paradigm. The workflow enactment service of grid workflow management systems may be built on

J. Cao et al. (Eds.): PAS 2014, CCIS 495, pp. 59–74, 2015.

top of the low level grid middleware (e.g. Globus toolkit [45] and UNICORE [51]), through which the workflow management system invokes services provided by grid resources. Some representative grid workflow systems include ASKALON [43], GrADS [45], GridAnt [45], Gridbus [46], GridFlow [45], Kepler [47], Pegasus [48], Taverna [49] and Triana [50]. In [59], comparisons of several representative Grid workflow systems are given in aspects of (1) scheduling architecture, (2) decision making, (3) planning scheme, (4) scheduling strategy, and (5) performance estimation. The work in [24] also conduct a survey about the support of temporal QoS (Quality of Service) in popular scientific workflow systems. In a scientific workflow system, at build-time stage, scientific processes are modeled or redesigned as workflow specifications which normally contain the process structure, the functional requirements for workflow activities and their non-functional requirements such as QoS constraints on time, cost, reliability, security and so on. At runtime stage, workflow instances are executed by employing the computing and data sharing ability of the underlying computing infrastructures and software services [27].

With the emerging of the latest cloud computing paradigm, the trend for distributed workflow systems is shifting to cloud computing based workflow systems, or cloud workflow systems for short. Given the advantages of cloud computing, cloud workflow systems are being widely used as platform software (or middleware services) to facilitate the usage of cloud services. In [44], CloudBus workflow management system deploys and manages job execution using Aneka which acts as a cloud middleware. In [41], using Montage on top of the Pegasus-WMS software, the authors investigate the differences between running scientific workflows on the cloud and on the grid. SwinDeW-C is a peer-to-peer based prototype cloud workflow system which is running on the SwinCloud cloud computing test bed mainly for scientific workflow applications such as pulsar searching [34]. Meanwhile, since Hadoop is almost a de facto standard for processing large datasets in the cloud, commercial public clouds such as Amazon Web Service and Microsoft Windows Azure have provided Hadoop clusters to enable scientific computing on the public cloud [1, 37].

Unlike traditional workflow systems which mainly invoke and execute software components using their own local software repository, scientific cloud workflow systems utilize software services in the cloud which are accessed through the Internet and executed at the service provider's infrastructure [4, 18]. A cloud workflow instance consists of many partially ordered cloud services, and probably from a number of different service providers. Therefore, the quality of a cloud workflow application is determined by the collective behaviors of all the cloud software services employed by the workflow application. Given the uncertainty lies in every cloud service, the quality of a cloud workflow instance becomes a much more complex combinatorial problem. Specifically, how to guarantee the delivery of satisfactory temporal QoS namely to achieve high on-time completion rate of scientific cloud workflows, is a big challenge [26]. This is because in the real world, scientific workflow normally stays in a temporal context and is often time constrained to achieve on-time completion of certain goals. For example, a weather forecast scientific workflow must be finished before the weather forecast program shown everyday, for instance, 6:00pm. A pulsar searching scientific workflow needs to be completed within 24 hours so as to meet the observation schedule of the telescope [32]. Failure of on-time completion will deteriorate the value of the workflow output.

In recent years, workflow temporal verification becomes the major approach for the assurance of temporal QoS and an important research topic in the workflow area [26]. As an important dimension of workflow QoS constraints, temporal constraints such as global deadlines and local milestones are often set at build time and verified at run time to ensure targeted on-time completion rate of scientific workflows. Workflow temporal verification, as one of the fundamental workflow system functionalities, is often implemented to monitor workflow runtime execution to maintain targeted temporal QoS [6]. However, given a large-scale data and computation intensive scientific workflow application and its dynamic cloud computing infrastructure, systematic investigation is required. Therefore, great efforts have been dedicated to the area of workflow temporal verification in recent years and it is high time that we should define the key research issues for scientific cloud workflows in order to keep our research on the right track.

The remainder of the paper is organized as follows. Section 2 presents a motivating example and then introduces a generic temporal verification framework with the four basic research issues and their state-of-the-art solutions. Section 3 further discusses the open challenges and presents some potential research directions. Section 4 introduces SwinDeW-V, an ongoing research project on temporal verification in our SwinDeW-C (**Swin**burne **De**centralized **W**orkflow for **C**loud) cloud workflow system. Finally, Section 5 addresses the conclusion.

2   Basic Research Issues

In this section, we first introduce a pulsar searching scientific workflow to illustrate the problem of temporal verification for scientific cloud workflows and further present a generic temporal verification framework with the four basic research issues.

2.1   Motivating Example and Problem Analysis

The pulsar searching process is a typical scientific workflow which involves a large number of data and computation intensive activities. For a typical single searching process, the average data volume is over 4 terabytes and the average execution time is about 23 hours on Swinburne high performance supercomputing facility. As described in [32], the pulsar searching process contains hundreds of high-level workflow activities and each may contain dozens or even more computation and data intensive tasks. For example, the data extraction and transfer sub-process may take about 1.5 hours, and the de-dispersion activity which is to counteract the effect of interstellar medium in the pulsar signals normally requires 13 hours. According to the research schedule, a single searching process is required to be completed within one day, i.e. 24 hours. However, since the average execution time of the whole process is about 23 hours and durations of most activities are very dynamic, it is very difficult to ensure on-time completion of such a process without effective monitoring and control mechanism.

Clearly, since human intervention is impossible for such a long-term process, software mechanism is required.

Based on the above motivating example, we can see that to ensure the on-time completion of a large-scale scientific cloud workflow is a challenging issue which requires a systematic solution. Temporal QoS can be measured by either the on-time completion rate or temporal violation rate. Clearly, the higher the on-time completion rate (or the lower the temporal violation rate), the better the temporal QoS is. In addition, there are two general requirements for scientific cloud workflow temporal verification which are *automation* and *cost-effectiveness*.

Automation: To speed up the execution, scientific workflow applications are designed to be as automatic as possible, so should be the temporal verification strategies. Besides, given such a large-scale workflow instances, human intervention is impossible for efficient and effective monitoring and control of workflow execution. We must rely on automatic software solutions.

Cost-effectiveness. In a cloud computing environment, every task for the workflow temporal verification incurs some cost. Here, the cost is generally referred to both monetary costs and time overheads. According to our observation, the total cost for temporal verification can grow dramatically with the increase of the workflow size. Therefore, we need to seriously consider cost effectiveness in every strategy design. Clearly, given similar temporal QoS (e.g. on-time completion rate), the smaller the total cost for temporal verification, the better the cost effectiveness is.

2.2   Basic Research Issues and State-of-the-Art Solutions

Based on the philosophy of "divide and conquer", a generic workflow QoS framework is proposed in [25] to provide a lifecycle QoS assurance in cloud workflow systems. Based on that, we can define a generic temporal verification framework which consists of four components including temporal constraint setting, temporal checkpoint selection, temporal verification and temporal violation handling. Clearly, how to design and implement these four components are the basic research issues. Here, we will introduce each of the components with their basic requirements and their representative and state-of-the-art solutions.

2.2.1   Research Issue #1: Temporal Constraints Setting

The first component of the framework is temporal constraint setting which deals with the negotiation of overall deadlines (as a part of the workflow specification) between customers and service providers, and the assignment of local temporal constraints to the local workflow segments or workflow activities for monitoring purpose[22]. Temporal constraints mainly include three types, viz. upper bound, lower bound and fixed-time [24]. Among them, an upper bound constraint is a relative time value so that the durations between two activities must be less than or equal to it. Upper bound constraints are the most general type of temporal constraints where the others can be transformed to its special cases. Therefore, upper bound constraints are the most widely used type of temporal constraints in workflow temporal verification.

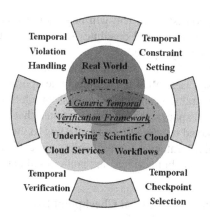

Fig. 1. A Generic Temporal Verification Framework for Scientific Cloud Workflows

The overall deadline is one of the most important QoS constraints for scientific cloud workflows. In addition, for recurrent workflow applications (namely those scientific workflow applications need to be repeated regularly), a SLA (Service Level Agreement) for on-time completion is also required to establish different levels of service quality (with different service prices) such as 90%, 99%, 99.9% and so on, similar to the SLA for cloud storage and computing services [1]. Furthermore, since a large-scale scientific cloud workflow may have a large number of activities and with complicate process structures, local temporal constraints for workflow segments or workflow activities are required to serve as the local milestones for monitoring purpose. Therefore, after the setting of the overall deadline and its SLA, the next step is the assignment of local temporal constraints.

Although temporal constraint setting only takes up a small effort in the temporal verification framework but it is clearly that the quality of the assigned temporal constraints will have significant effect on the subsequent steps. For example, if the overall deadline is too tight, the chance that the targeted SLA can be met will be very small regardless the subsequent monitoring and control strategies. In contrast, if the assigned milestones are too flexible, the effectiveness of workflow monitoring will be significantly deteriorated. Therefore, temporal constraint setting needs to consider the trade-off between user requirements (e.g. workflow time and budget) and the system performance (e.g. service response time and price). Meanwhile, the overall deadline and the local temporal constraints need to be consistent so that the final on-time completion can be achieved with the progressively success of local milestones.

Generally speaking, there are two basic ways to assign QoS constraints, one is activity-level assignment and the other is workflow-level assignment. Since the whole workflow process is composed of all individual activities, an overall workflow-level constraint can be obtained by the composition of activity-level constraints. On the contrary, activity-level constraints can also be assigned by the decomposition of workflow-level constraints [59]. The issue of automatically translating the overall deadline into deadlines for the individual subtasks is investigated in [8, 21]. In [22], based on a probabilistic temporal consistency model, a workflow temporal constraint setting strategy which consists of a win-win negotiation process between customers and service providers for the overall deadline, and an automatic propagation process for local deadlines, has been proposed.

The state-of-the-art solution for workflow temporal constraint management is proposed in [24]. In most cases, after the setting of temporal constraints at workflow build-time stage, temporal constraints as a type of QoS requirements cannot be changed. However, in this paper, the authors suggested that local temporal constraints can be dynamically relaxed or strengthened according to the runtime workflow execution states. Accordingly, strategies for probability time deficit/redundancy propagation process for activities on both critical and non-critical paths have been proposed.

2.2.2   Research Issue #2: Temporal Checkpoint Selection

Temporal checkpoints are the decision points for further actions such as temporal verification and temporal violation handling in the temporal verification framework. Therefore, checkpoint selection plays a critical role in the whole temporal verification framework since the number of selected checkpoints basically determines the possible number of times for temporal verification and temporal violation handling. Since it is normally too expensive to conduct temporal verification at every activity point but insufficient to conduct temporal verification only at a few pre-defined activity points, the target of a checkpoint selection strategy (CSS) is to select only essential activity points where potential temporal violations can be detected. In such a case, the cost of temporal verification and possible temporal violation handling can be minimized.

In recent years, many checkpoint selection strategies, from intuitive rule based to sophisticated model based, have been proposed. The work in [17] takes every workflow activity as a checkpoint. The work in [35] selects the start activity as a checkpoint and adds a new checkpoint after each decision activity is executed. It also mentions a type of static activity point which is defined by users at the build-time stage. The work in [9] selects an activity as a checkpoint if its execution time exceeds the maximum duration while the work in [10] selects an activity as a checkpoint if its execution time exceeds the mean duration. The first checkpoint selection strategy which satisfies the property of necessity and sufficiency (which is regarded as the benchmark for temporal checkpoint selection) is proposed in [6] where minimum time redundancies for SC (Strong Consistency) and WC (Weak Consistency) are defined. Here, necessity means that only those activity points where intermediate temporal violations take place are selected and sufficiency means that there are no any omitted activity points. For example, an activity point is selected as a WC checkpoint if and only if its execution time is larger than the sum of its mean duration and its minimum WC time redundancy. The comparison result shows that with the measurement of necessity and sufficiency, the one based on minimum time redundancy has outperformed all the other checkpoint selection strategies.

The state-of-the-art checkpoint selection strategy is proposed in [7] where the authors investigate the temporal dependency between different upper bound temporal constraints. The results have shown that at any specific checkpoint, for those temporal constraints which cover the checkpoint and have the same type of temporal dependency, such as SC (Strong Consistency) temporal dependency, temporal verification is needed once only to verify all of them. Therefore, many times of unnecessary temporal verification are avoided.

2.2.3 Research Issue #3: Temporal Verification

As one of the major dimensions of software verification whose goal is to assure that software fully satisfies all the expected requirements, temporal verification is to assure that workflow applications satisfy temporal constraints. Specifically, according to a temporal consistency model, temporal verification is to check whether the current temporal consistency state of the runtime workflow application satisfies its build-time specification. Temporal verification is usually conducted after a checkpoint is selected. The original task of temporal verification has two steps. The first step is to check the current temporal consistency state so as to determine whether a specific type of temporal violation has occurred. The second step (after a temporal violation is detected) is to calculate the time deficits (the time delays at the current checkpoint given different temporal constraints) and other runtime information to facilitate the temporal violation handling (i.e. a time deficit compensation process) of temporal violations.

Traditionally, there are only binary states of consistency or inconsistency defined by the temporal consistency model. However, as stated in [5], it argues that the conventional consistency condition is too restrictive and covers several different states which should be handled differently for the purpose of cost effectiveness. Therefore, it divides conventional inconsistency into Weak Consistency (WC), Weak Inconsistency (WI) and Strong Inconsistency (SI) and treats them accordingly. However, multiple-state based temporal consistency model cannot support quantitative measurement of temporal consistency states and lacks the ability to support statistical analysis. Therefore in [22], a probability based build-time temporal consistency model is presented to facilitate the setting of temporal constraints. Different from previous discrete temporal consistency model such as binary-state or multiple-state, the probability based temporal consistency model is a type of continuous-state model where the temporal consistency state is measured using the probability confidence for on-time completion such as 90% or 80%. The runtime version of the probability based temporal consistency model is proposed in [33] to facilitate runtime temporal checkpoint selection and verification.

Due to the significant closeness between temporal checkpoint selection and temporal verification, they are often referred as temporal consistency monitoring in many studies [25, 26]. Therefore, the state-of-the-art temporal verification strategy can be regarded as the combined strategy of the temporal dependency based checkpoint selection strategy and the temporal verification strategy with the probability based temporal consistency model, which is proposed in [28].

2.2.4 Research Issue #4: Temporal Violation Handling

If temporal violations are detected after temporal verification, temporal violation handling strategies will be requested. The work in [52] introduces five types of workflow exceptions where temporal violations can be classified into deadline expiry. However, it should be noted that what we detected and handled temporal violations are intermediate temporal violations rather than final violations which are beyond recovery. The work in [53] proposes three alternate courses of recovery action being no action (NIL), rollback (RBK) and compensation (COM). NIL, which entirely counts on the automatic recovery of the system itself, is normally not considered 'risk-free'. As for RBK, unlike handling conventional system function failures, it normally causes extra delays and makes the current temporal violations even worse. In contrast, COM, namely time deficit compensation, is a suitable approach for handling temporal violations. The work in [5] proposes a time deficit allocation (TDA) strategy which compensates current time deficits by utilizing the expected time redundancy of subsequent activities. However, since the time deficit is not truly reduced by TDA, this strategy can only postpone the violations of local constraints on some local workflow segments, but has no effectiveness on the overall deadlines. Therefore, we need to investigate those strategies which can indeed reduce the time deficits. Besides many others, one of the compensation processes which is often employed and can actually make up the time deficit is workflow rescheduling.

Workflow rescheduling, such as local rescheduling (which deals with the mapping of underling resources to workflow activities within specific local workflow segments), is normally triggered by the violation of QoS constraints [13, 61]. Workflow scheduling as well as workflow rescheduling are classical NP-complete problems [11, 16]. Therefore, many heuristic and metaheuristic algorithms are proposed. The work in [60] has presented a systematic overview of workflow scheduling algorithms for scientific grid computing. The work in [12] proposes an ACO (Ant Colony Optimization) approach to address scientific workflow scheduling problems with various QoS requirements such as reliability constraints, makespan constraints and cost constraints. For handling temporal violations in scientific cloud workflow systems, both time and cost need to be considered while time has a priority over cost since we focus more on reducing the time deficits during the compensation process. An ACO based local workflow rescheduling strategy is proposed by us in [30] for handling temporal violations in scientific workflows.

Another issue about violation handling is that some violations may be beyond the handling power of certain violation handling strategies. Therefore, considering the handling capability, statistically recoverable and non-recoverable temporal violations are defined in [23] so that they can be handled properly with different violation handling strategies. While statistically recoverable temporal violations can usually be recovered by workflow rescheduling strategies, statistically non-recoverable temporal violations can only be recovered by heavy-weight (i.e. more expensive) solutions such as resource recruitment, stop and restart, processor swapping and workflow restructure [26]. The state-of-the-art work on a general temporal violation handling framework is proposed in [31] where K levels of temporal violations can be defined according to the handling capability of K available violation handling strategies. In such a case, a temporal violation can be handled by the violation handling strategy which has enough capability but with the least cost. Therefore, the total violation handling cost can be minimized.

In addition, to reduce the increasing violation handling cost, the work in [28] proposed a novel concept of "violation handling point selection" which is to further select a subset of checkpoints for violation handling from the set of necessary and sufficient checkpoints for temporal verification. Traditionally, scientific workflow temporal verification adopts the philosophy that to maintain satisfactory temporal QoS, similar to the handling of functional exceptions, temporal violation handling should be triggered on every necessary and sufficient temporal checkpoint [33]. However, there is a common but overlooked phenomenon that the execution delay may often be small enough so that the saved execution time of the subsequent workflow activities could automatically compensate for it. In [28], an adaptive violation handling point selection strategy is proposed to fully utilize this kind of "*self-recovery*" phenomenon to significantly reduce the number of violation handling points, so as to reduce the temporal total violation handling cost.

3   Open Challenges

As discussed in Section 2, a clear research roadmap for scientific cloud workflow temporal verification is to follow the generic temporal verification framework and investigate new strategies for each component. Although temporal verification for scientific workflows has been extensively studied in the last few years, there are still many open challenges especially brought by the shift of the computing paradigm from conventional cluster or grid to the cloud. However, since not every researcher needs to follow the generic framework and they may only be interested in the studies of one of the components, we try to focus on three major and high-level open challenges in this paper instead of discussing the very specific tasks for each component in this section. For each open challenge, we will discuss its problems and try to point out some potential research directions with preliminary results if available. Specifically, there are three major open challenges as follows.

3.1   Open Challenge #1: The Forecasting Strategy for Scientific Cloud Workflow Activity Durations

The accurate modeling and estimation of activity durations is very important to the effectiveness of temporal verification. However, this is not a trivial issue in a cloud environment. Traditional scientific workflow systems are often deployed in community based computing environment such as clusters and grids where resources are usually reserved in advance and "best-effort" based QoS strategy are adopted [40]. In such a case, the performance of the underlying computing resources is relatively stable and thus the activity durations can be modeled with reasonable accuracy with simple statistic models [22]. Some advanced forecasting strategies based on time-series patterns and CPU trend analysis have been proved to be very effective for scientific workflows[2, 58]. In contrast, cloud is a multitenant computing environment and dynamic resource provisioning is often required to guarantee the target service quality purchased by the users. Therefore, the underlying resources are dynamically changing and hence their performance is hard to predict. In addition, traditional forecasting strategies mainly concern with the computing time of the workflow activities.

However, as analyzed in some literatures, there are many other time overheads in scientific workflows [42] and they may become significant in the cloud computing environment such as data transfer. In fact, as the datasets in scientific workflows are usually very big, the data transfer time for large datasets across different data centers through the Internet can be enormous. Therefore, we need to investigate these time attributes and include them to the forecasting model.

There are a few papers investigating the modeling and estimation of cloud service response time. Specifically, queueing model is employed as the basic forecasting tool as it is powerful in modeling a multitenant cloud environment [19]. In addition, there are some studies on the data transfer in a cloud environment and also some data placement strategies to reduce the data transfer time for scientific cloud workflows [62]. Nevertheless, the forecasting strategy for scientific cloud workflow activity durations is still an open challenge and it is one of the fundamental issues for scientific cloud workflow temporal verification.

3.2   Open Challenge #2: The Monitoring of Many Parallel Computing Tasks

MapReduce kind of parallel data processing is pervasive in both scientific and business workflow applications [14, 36]. In business workflow applications, the parallelism is mainly at the workflow-level, namely a large number of business workflow instances each representing a unique customer request. However, in scientific workflow applications, the parallelism is mainly at the activity-level or even inside each activity at the algorithm-level [3]. As current scientific workflow temporal verification focuses on the critical path, such low-level parallelism can usually be simplified as a compound workflow activity for the ease of monitoring and the loss of accuracy is negligible [33]. However, as cloud computing is the becoming the major platform for scientific computing, MapReduce kind of programming model will help to exploit the benefits of massive parallelism to improve the efficiency of scientific cloud workflows. Therefore, we can envisage the increasing popularity of parallel data processing in scientific computing and hence the increase of parallel structures in scientific cloud workflow applications. In such a case, we can no longer treat them as sequential structures but to provide new monitoring strategies for many parallel computing tasks.

Recently, there are a few studies on the monitoring of large number of parallel business workflows which may provide a reference for the monitoring of many parallel computing tasks in scientific workflows. The work in [29] proposes a novel idea where system time points instead of traditional activity points are selected as temporal checkpoints. Accordingly, the system throughput instead of traditional response time is adopted as the measurement for system performance. However, as mentioned above, business workflows and scientific workflows have different levels of parallelism, and hence the strategy for monitoring parallel business workflow instances at the workflow-level may not be suitable for monitoring parallel computing tasks at the activity-level. One of the major differences is that there is significant data and time dependency in scientific workflows at the activity-level but much less in business workflows at the workflow-level. Therefore, how to extend the current scientific workflow temporal verification strategies to effectively monitor many parallel computing tasks is an open challenge.

3.3 Open Challenge #3: Temporal Violation Handling for Scientific Cloud Workflows

Generally speaking, the objective for handling intermediate temporal violations in scientific workflows is to reduce the response time of the subsequent workflow activities so as to compensate for the existing time deficit. In the conventional resource environments such as cluster and grid, it is very expensive and time consuming to add new resources such as virtual machines during workflow runtime. Therefore, we try to utilize existing resources as much as possible with workflow rescheduling strategies. However, without additional resources, some serious temporal violations may not be able to be recovered. Meanwhile, due to the change of the local schedule, the tasks of other workflow instances will also be affected and even violate their temporal constraints. Therefore, there is obvious limitation in the conventional handling strategies. The emergence of cloud computing can totally change such a situation. Currently, in most public clouds, virtual machines can be easily provisioned in less than 30 seconds. In addition, many public clouds such as Amazon Web Service provide discounted prices for reserved virtual machines and even bidding prices for spot instances to further reduce the cost for dynamic provisioning. Therefore, it is now becoming acceptable in both time and cost to add new resources at workflow runtime.

There are some literatures reporting the time for starting new virtual machines in popular public clouds [38, 39]. The results for much more benchmarks on the performance of computing, storage and network services in public clouds can be found at [20]. However, for handling temporal violations, we need to not only consider the time overheads for adding new resources but also the time overheads for data and task re-allocation between the existing and new resources. It is necessary to estimate the cost of the handling strategy and then make smart trade-off between violation handling and the intermediate temporal violations. Therefore, it is still an open challenge for the design of efficient and cost-effective violation handing strategies for scientific cloud workflows.

4   SwinDeW-V Research Project

SwinDeW-V is an ongoing research project and part of the Swinburne Cloud Infrastructure. SwinDeW-V focuses on temporal verification and serves as one of the key functionalities in our SwinDeW-C cloud workflow system [34]. In this section, we introduce the system implementation of the temporal verification framework in our SwinDeW-C cloud workflow system.

SwinDeW-C (Swinburne Decentralised Workflow for Cloud) is located within SwinGrid environment which contains many computing nodes distributed in different places. Each grid node contains many computers including high performance PCs and/or supercomputers composed of significant numbers of computing units. Swin-DeW-C is currently running at Swinburne University of Technology as a virtualized environment which is physically composed of 10 servers and 10 high-end PCs at the Swinburne Astrophysics Supercomputer Node. To simulate the cloud computing environment, we set up VMware [56] software on the physical servers and create virtual clusters as datacenters. For more details, please refer to [27].

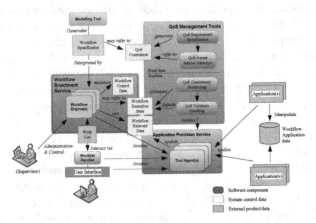

Fig. 2. SwinDeW-C System Architecture [27]

As depicted in Figure 2, the architecture of SwinDeW-C is designed according to classical WfMC reference model [57] . The four basic components of temporal verification framework are implemented as part of the workflow QoS management tools in SwinDeW-C. Specifically, the QoS management tools include QoS requirement specification, QoS-aware service selection, QoS consistency monitoring and QoS violation handling, and they are designed as generic and open components to meet different QoS requirements such as time, cost, reliability, security and so on. For our temporal verification framework, temporal constraint setting is part of QoS requirement specification and QoS-aware service selection which are mainly interacted with the workflow modelling tool to create workflow specifications. The QoS requirement specification component will generate the QoS constraints including the temporal constraints, which are part of the workflow specification and the basic reference data for QoS-aware service selection. The QoS-aware service selection component will return the available (best and backup) software services satisfying the QoS constraints, through the broker service (part of the application provision services). After the workflow specifications are submitted to the workflow enactment services, the workflow instances can be executed by invoking software services which are managed by the tool agents. The tool agents will in charge for the data communication between the workflow system and the software services which are either available in the system local repository or delivered by outside service providers in the cloud market. During runtime execution stage, the workflow execution state will be constantly monitored by the QoS consistency monitoring component which includes temporal checkpoint selection and temporal verification. The workflow execution state can be displayed by a watch list which contains runtime information such as time submitted, time finished, percentage of completion, service status and many other real-time and possible statistic data. When the QoS violations such as temporal violations are detected, alter messages will be sent to the QoS violation handling component. The QoS violation handling component which includes the temporal violation handling strategies will analyze the workflow execution state and the QoS requirement specification to decide further actions such as workflow rescheduling and additional resource recruitment through the interactions with the application provision services.

Currently, SwinDeW-V has provided fully support for high temporal QoS for scientific workflows [26]. In the future, SwinDeW-V will explore more on the support for business cloud workflows. Specifically, those open issues proposed in Section 3 need to be further investigated. Our ultimate objective is that SwinDeW-V can be developed as an independent software component which can be easily adopted by any cloud workflow systems including both scientific and business cloud workflows to facilitate the functionalities of the temporal verification framework.

5   Conclusion

Workflow temporal verification is the major approach to guarantee the on-time completion of workflow applications. In the last few years, a lot of research efforts have been dedicated to the temporal verification in scientific workflow systems. However, with the emergence of cloud computing, there are some open challenges for the temporal verification in scientific cloud workflow systems. In this paper, through the introduction of a generic temporal verification framework, four basic research issues for scientific cloud workflow temporal verification including temporal constraint setting, temporal checkpoint selection, temporal verification and temporal violation handling were first presented with representative and state-of-the-art solutions. These four basic research issues can lay out a clear research road map for scientific cloud workflow temporal verification. Afterwards, three open research challenges including the forecasting strategy for scientific cloud workflow activity durations, the monitoring of many parallel computing tasks, and temporal violation handling for scientific cloud workflows are discussed with the introduction of some potential research directions. This paper provided a systematic overview of the current research work and some open challenges for scientific cloud workflows temporal verification in the future. The result of this paper is useful for those researchers who are interested in time related quality assurance in scientific cloud workflow systems.

Acknowledgement. The research work reported in this paper is partly supported by National Natural Science Foundation of China (NSFC) under No. 61300042 and No. 61321064, Shanghai Knowledge Service Platform Project No. ZF1213.

References

[1] Amazon EC2, http://aws.amazon.com/ec2/ (accessed on September 1, 2014)

[2] Akioka, S., Muraoka, Y.: Extended Forecast of CPU and Network Load on Computational Grid. In: Proc. 2004 IEEE International Symposium on Cluster Computing and the Grid, pp. 765–772 (2004)

[3] Barga, R., Gannon, D.: Scientific versus Business Workflows. In: Workflows for e-Science (2007)

[4] Buyya, R., Yeo, C.S., Venugopal, S.: Market-Oriented Cloud Computing: Vision, Hype, and Reality for Delivering IT Services as Computing Utilities. In: Proc. 10th IEEE International Conference on High Performance Computing and Communications (2008)

[5] Chen, J., Yang, Y.: Multiple States based Temporal Consistency for Dynamic Verification of Fixed-time Constraints in Grid Workflow Systems. Concurrency and Computation: Practice and Experience 19(7), 965–982 (2007)

[6] Chen, J., Yang, Y.: Adaptive Selection of Necessary and Sufficient Checkpoints for Dynamic Verification of Temporal Constraints in Grid Workflow Systems. ACM Trans. on Auto. and Adapt. Sys. 2(2) (2007)

[7] Chen, J., Yang, Y.: Temporal Dependency based Checkpoint Selection for Dynamic Verification of Temporal Constraints in Scientific Workflow Systems. ACM Transactions on Software Engineering and Methodology 20(3), Article 9 (2011)

[8] Chen, J., Yang, Y.: Localising Temporal Constraints in Scientific Workflows. Journal of Computer and System Sciences 76(6), 464–474 (2010)

[9] Chen, J., Yang, Y., Chen, T.Y.: Dynamic Verification of Temporal Constraints on-the-fly for Workflow Systems. In: Proc. the 11th Asia-Pacific Software Engineering Conference, pp. 30–37 (2004)

[10] Chen, J., Yang, Y.: Activity Completion Duration Based Checkpoint Selection for Dynamic Verification of Temporal Constraints in Grid Workflow Systems. Int. J. High Perform. Comput. Appl. 22(3), 319–329 (2008)

[11] Chen, W., Zhang, J., Yu, Y.: Workflow Scheduling in Grids: An Ant Colony Optimization Approach. In: Proc. 2007 IEEE Congress on Evolutionary Computation, pp. 3308–3315 (2007)

[12] Chen, W., Zhang, J.: An Ant Colony Optimization Approach to a Grid Workflow Scheduling Problem With Various QoS Requirements. IEEE Transactions on Systems, Man, and Cybernetics, Part C: Applications and Reviews 39(1), 29–43 (2009)

[13] Cooper, K., Dasgupta, A., Kennedy, K., Koelbel, C., Mandal, A.: New Grid Scheduling and Rescheduling Methods in the GrADS Project. In: Proc. 18th International Parallel and Distributed Processing Symposium, pp. 199–206 (2004)

[14] Dean, J., Ghemawat, S.: Mapreduce: Simplified Data Processing on Large Clusters. Communications of the ACM 51(1), 107–113 (2008)

[15] Deelman, E., Gannon, D., Shields, M., Taylor, I.: Workflows and e-Science: An Overview of Workflow System Features and Capabilities. Fut. Gene. Comp. Syst. 25(5), 528–540 (2009)

[16] Dou, W., Zhao, J., Fan, S.: A Collaborative Scheduling Approach for Service-Driven Scientific Workflow Execution. Journal of Computer and System Sciences 76(6), 416–427 (2010)

[17] Eder, J., Panagos, E., Rabinovich, M.: Time Constraints in Workflow Systems. In: Jarke, M., Oberweis, A. (eds.) CAiSE 1999. LNCS, vol. 1626, pp. 286–300. Springer, Heidelberg (1999)

[18] Foster, I., Yong, Z., Raicu, I., Lu, S.: Cloud Computing and Grid Computing 360-Degree Compared. In: Proc. 2008 Grid Computing Environments Workshop, pp. 1–10 (2008)

[19] Hamzeh, K.: Performance Analysis of Cloud Computing Centers Using M/G/m/m+r Queuing Systems. IEEE Transactions on Parallel and Distributed Systems 23(5), 936–943 (2012)

[20] Cloud Harmony, http://cloudharmony.com/ (accessed on September 1, 2014)

[21] Kao, B., Garcia-Molina, H.: Deadline Assignment in a Distributed Soft Real-Time System. IEEE Trans. Parallel Distrib. Syst. 8(12), 1268–1274 (1997)

[22] Liu, X., Chen, J., Yang, Y.: A Probabilistic Strategy for Setting Temporal Constraints in Scientific Workflows. In: Dumas, M., Reichert, M., Shan, M.-C. (eds.) BPM 2008. LNCS, vol. 5240, pp. 180–195. Springer, Heidelberg (2008)

[23] Liu, X., Chen, J., Wu, Z., Ni, Z., Yuan, D., Yang, Y.: Handling Recoverable Temporal Violations in Scientific Workflow Systems: A Workflow Rescheduling Based Strategy. In: Proc. 10th IEEE/ACM International Symposium on Cluster, Cloud and Grid Computing, pp. 534–537 (2010)

[24] Liu, X., Ni, Z., Chen, J., Yang, Y.: A Probabilistic Strategy for Temporal Constraint Management in Scientific Workflow Systems. Concurrency and Computation: Practice and Experience 23(16), 1893–1919 (2011)

[25] Liu, X., Yang, Y., Yuan, D., Zhang, G., Li, W., Cao, D.: A Generic QoS Framework for Cloud Workflow Systems. In: Proc. International Conference on Cloud and Green Computing, pp. 713–720 (2011)

[26] Liu, X., Chen, J., Yang, Y.: Temporal QoS Management in Scientific Cloud Workflow Systems. Elsevier (2012)

[27] Liu, X., Yuan, D., Zhang, G., Li, W., Cao, D., He, Q., Chen, J., Yang, Y.: The Design of Cloud Workflow Systems. Springer (2012)

[28] Liu, X., Yang, Y., Yuan, D., Chen, J.: Do We Need to Handle Every Temporal Violation in Scientific Workflow Systems? ACM Trans. on Soft. Eng. and Method. 23(1), Article 5 (2014)

[29] Liu, X., Yang, Y., Cao, D., Yuan, D.: Selecting Checkpoints along the Time Line: A Novel Temporal Checkpoint Selection Strategy for Monitoring a Batch of Parallel Business Processes. In: Proc. 35th International Conference on Software Engineering (NIER Track), pp. 1281–1284 (2013)

[30] Liu, X., Ni, Z., Wu, Z., Yuan, D., Chen, J., Yang, Y.: An Effective Framework of Light-Weight Handling for Three-Level Fine-Grained Recoverable Temporal Violations in Scientific Workflows. In: Proc. 16th IEEE International Conference on Parallel and Distributed Systems, pp. 43–50 (2010)

[31] Liu, X., Ni, Z., Wu, Z., Yuan, D., Chen, J., Yang, Y.: A Novel General Framework for Automatic and Cost-Effective Handling of Recoverable Temporal Violations in Scientific Workflow Systems. Journal of Systems and Software 84(3), 492–509 (2011)

[32] Liu, X., Ni, Z., Yuan, D., Jiang, Y., Wu, Z., Chen, J., Yang, Y.: A Novel Statistical Time-Series Pattern based Interval Forecasting Strategy for Activity Durations in Workflow Systems. Journal of Systems and Software 84(3), 354–376 (2011)

[33] Liu, X., Yang, Y., Jiang, Y., Chen, J.: Preventing Temporal Violations in Scientific Workflows: Where and How. IEEE Transactions on Software Engineering 37(6), 805–825 (2011)

[34] Liu, X., Yuan, D., Zhang, G., Chen, J., Yang, Y.: SwinDeW-C: A Peer-to-Peer Based Cloud Workflow System. In: Furht, B., Escalante, A. (eds.) Handbook of Cloud Computing. Springer (2010)

[35] Marjanovic, O., Orlowska, M.E.: On Modelling and Verification of Temporal Constraints in Production Workflows. Knowledge and Information Systems 1(2), 157–192 (1999)

[36] Matsunaga, A., Tsugawa, M., Fortes, J.: CloudBLAST: Combining MapReduce and Virtualization on Distributed Resources for Bioinformatics Applications. In: Proc. 4th IEEE International Conference on e-Science, pp. 222–229 (2008)

[37] Windows Azure, http://www.microsoft.com/windowsazure/ (accessed on September 1, 2014)

[38] Ming, M., Humphrey, M.: A Performance Study on the VM Startup Time in the Cloud. In: Proc. 5th IEEE International Conference on Cloud Computing, pp. 423–430 (2012)

[39] Moldovan, D., Copil, G., Hong-Linh, T., Dustdar, S.: MELA: Monitoring and Analyzing Elasticity of Cloud Services. In: Proc. 5th IEEE International Conference on Cloud Computing Technology and Science, vol. 1, pp. 80–87 (2013)

[40] Netto, M.A.S., Bubendorfer, K., Buyya, R.: SLA-Based Advance Reservations with Flexible and Adaptive Time QoS Parameters. In: Krämer, B.J., Lin, K.-J., Narasimhan, P. (eds.) ICSOC 2007. LNCS, vol. 4749, pp. 119–131. Springer, Heidelberg (2007)

[41] Hoffa, C., Mehta, G., Freeman, T., Deelman, E., Keahey, K., Berriman, B., Good, J.: On the Use of Cloud Computing for Scientific Workflows. In: Proc. 4th IEEE International Conference on e-Science, pp. 640–645 (2008)

[42] Prodan, R., Fahringer, T.: Overhead Analysis of Scientific Workflows in Grid Environments. IEEE Transactions on Parallel and Distributed Systems 19(3), 378–393 (2008)

[43] Askalon Project, http://www.dps.uibk.ac.at/projects/askalon (accessed on September 1, 2014)

[44] CloudBus Project, http://www.cloudbus.org/ (accessed on September 1, 2014)

[45] GridAnt Project, http://www.globus.org/cog/projects/gridant/ (accessed on September 1, 2014)

[46] GridBus Project, http://www.gridbus.org (accessed on September 1, 2014)

[47] Kepler Project, http://kepler-project.org/ (accessed on September 1, 2014)

[48] Pegasus Project, http://pegasus.isi.edu/ (accessed on September 1, 2014)

[49] Taverna Project, http://www.mygrid.org.uk/tools/taverna/ (accessed on September 1, 2014)

[50] Triana Project, http://www.trianacode.org/ (accessed on September 1, 2014)

[51] UNICORE Project, http://www.unicore.eu/ (accessed on September 1, 2014)

[52] Russell, N., van der Aalst, W.M.P., ter Hofstede, A.H.M.: Exception Handling Patterns in Process-Aware Information Systems. Technical Report BPM-06-04, BPMcen-ter.org (2006)

[53] Russell, N., van der Aalst, W.M.P., ter Hofstede, A.H.M.: Workflow Exception Patterns. In: Martinez, F.H., Pohl, K. (eds.) CAiSE 2006. LNCS, vol. 4001, pp. 288–302. Springer, Heidelberg (2006)

[54] Scientific Workflows Survey, http://www.extreme.indiana.edu/swf-survey/ (accessed on September 1, 2014)

[55] Taylor, I.J., Deelman, E., Gannon, D.B., Shields, M.: Workflows for e-Science: Scientific Workflows for Grids (2007)

[56] VMware, http://www.vmware.com/ (accessed on September 1, 2014)

[57] Workflow Coalition Management, The Workflow Reference Model. Technical Report WFMC-TC-1003 (1995)

[58] Liu, X., Chen, J., Liu, K., Yang, Y.: Forecasting Duration Intervals of Scientific Workflow Activities Based on Time-Series Patterns. In: Proc. 2008 IEEE Fourth International Conference on eScience, pp. 23–30 (2008)

[59] Yu, J., Buyya, R.: A Taxonomy of Workflow Management Systems for Grid Computing. Journal of Grid Computing (3), 171–200 (2005)

[60] Yu, J., Buyya, R.: Workflow Scheduling Algorithms for Grid Computing. Technical Report GRIDS-TR-2007-10, The University of Melbourne, Australia (2007)

[61] Yu, Z., Shi, W.: An Adaptive Rescheduling Strategy for Grid Workflow Applications. In: Proc. 2007 IEEE International Symposium on Parallel and Distributed Processing (IPDPS 2007), pp. 115–122 (2007)

[62] Yuan, D., Yang, Y., Liu, X., Chen, J.: A Data Placement Strategy in Scientific Cloud Workflows. Future Generation Computer Systems 26(6), 1200–1214 (2010)

Quality Control Method in Crowdsourcing Platform for Professional Dictionary Compilation Process (PDCCP)

Shanshan Feng[1], Xiao Li[2], and Huisi Ou[1]

[1] Department of CSE
Shanghai Jiao Tong University
{fswl6869,ogerhsou}@sjtu.edu.cn
[2] Department of CS
University of Southern California
lixiao@hotmail.com

Abstract. Crowdsourcing as a new popular technology is being considered as an efficient way to accomplish many tasks in people's lives. Quality control for crowdsoucing consequentially becomes an essential topic to ensure the task's final performance. In this paper, we introduced a crowdsourcing platform for professional dictionary compilation (PDCCP), which involves words translation and audition and features a large-scale non-computing automatic crowdsourcing task type. Especially for this kind, we proposed a Quality Testing Method working appropriately in PDCCP. Basically, in the quality testing part of the original translation crowdsroucing task, we used another crowdsourcing task to complete the audition process and returned the audition results as translation task results and also feedbacks of task attendants' submitted results quality. To further improve the quality contorl method in PDCCP and take advantage of the Quality Testing Method's feedback, we explored two task distribution strategies, which are static strategy and competency strategy, and we also expeirmented how these strategies might influnece the task's quality and efficiency.

Keywords: Crowdsourcing, Quality testing method, Task distribution strategy.

1   Introduction

With the development of Internet technology and the advent of big data era, topics based on large scale and how people could better utilize them became upsurge. Crowdsourcing, as a new technology applied to production, is a rising star during recent years [1][7][8][9][10] . It refers to a process that companies or organizations freely distribute their tasks that are originally completed by employees to public networks [2]. The core of crowdsourcing is to reach a goal by integrating and taking advantage of large-scale and easy-accessing resources. Company can improve task's completion efficiency and cut down task's cost by using crowdsourcing technology.

J. Cao et al. (Eds.): PAS 2014, CCIS 495, pp. 75–92, 2015.

However, due to the uncertainty of solution providers, the quality of results obtained by crowdsourcing is hard to guarantee, which might cause further problems and require extra work, making crowdsourcing lost its advantage of costs and efficiency. Depending on different tasks of crowdsourcing, task quality may also influenced by other factors, such as the difficulty of seeking the effective quality testing methods, the unreasonable designed task model and etc.

In this paper, we introduced a crowdsourcing platform for professional dictionary compilation (PDCCP) and mainly focused on quality control part in it. Our contributions include: (1) proposed a specific quality testing method for quality control in PDCCP, (2) experimented some task distribution strategies in PDCCP. We also compared other related quality control methods in the next section and analyze the experiment result in Section 6.

2   Related Work

2.1   Gold Standard Test

Gold standard test [3] in medical and statistic field means the best diagnostic test or standard testing program under reasonable condition or the most accurate test in any conditions. In crowdsourcing quality testing, companies can mix Gold Standard Data with crowdsourcing subtasks and distribute them normally to task attendants. Within the submitted results from test attendants, the completed quality of Gold Standard Data can be judged directly. By comparing test attendants' submitted results with Gold Standard Data's accomplishing results, companies can measure the general quality of the subtask's results. To some degree, task quality testing's accuracy and recall rate is proportional to the ratio of Gold Standard Data in the task. In addition, in Gold Standard Test, company should not let task attendants be aware of the existence of Gold Standard Data. Otherwise this method will not be effective.

The advantage of this quality testing method is that the algorithm is simple and easy to achieve. If the Gold Standard Data is well designed, it can assure definite accuracy. Nonetheless, this quality testing method highly rely on the Gold Standard Data, which means Gold Standard Data must be prepared before the crowdsourcing task start; thus increased task time and cost. Furthermore, seeking Gold Standard Data for some crowdsourcing tasks is impractical such as crowdsourcing tasks involving creativity. Therefore, the usage of Gold Standard Test is restricted.

2.2   The Expectation-Maximization Algorithm with Separation of Bias and Errors

In 1997, Arthur Dempster, Nan Laird and Donald Rubin in their thesis [4] proposed Expectation Maximization Algorithm that using iteration method to find unobservable hidden variables that are important element in statistics models. Panagiotis G. Ipeirotis, Foster Provost, and Jing Wang [5] from New York University then claim that directly using Expectation Maximization Algorithm's application to crowdsourcing tasks is not quite appropriate. This is because crowdsourcing task need a lot judgments and consideration from task attendants. Due to their various knowledge levels, abilities, experiences or other aspects, the submitted results for crowdsourcing task have judgment bias. They suggested that we should distinct (unrecoverable) errors from (recoverable) bias and then proposed an Expectation Maximization Algorithm with separation of bias and errors especially for crowdsourcing task.

Error means a task attendant submitted meaningless and false task results. Its accuracy is quite the same as computer randomly submitted task results. These are mostly from deceptive task attendants. For instance, submitting same answer for all task questions or randomly choosing answers for each question. Bias means a task attendant's submitted biased task results due to some specified reasons. By some methods, company can effectively use these biased information and improve the accuracy of quality testing. Factors causing bias are different perceptions of people's personal standard, spiteful inverse answer submitted etc.

Therefore, perfect task attendants and spiteful attackers with simple strategy are both valuable since their revising cost is approximately 0; however, for unified submitters or random submitters, their revising cost is relatively high. Thus, it's not necessary for us to expect task attendants have very high accuracy. As long as task attendant's revising cost is low enough and its bias is predictable and revisable, then those attendants' results can be accepted.

In some online crowdsourcing tasks, there exists task attendants that are seriously contribute their efforts but receive low quality grade for their submitted results due to the disregard of bias from errors. These actually high quality task attendants are alienated from or even quit in the middle of some crowdsourcing tasks that simply using mode for judgment. Expectation Maximization Algorithm with Separation of Bias and Errors can effectively solve this situation.

This algorithm is completed entirely by computer and it does not need prepare any extra information. In addition, it can obtain task quality and distinguish bias among task attendants at the same time. However, this algorithm has following limitations: (1) Quality testing results are mostly depend on quality of the task attendants, if the proportion of low quality attendants are relatively large, algorithm results do not work well. This usually appears in small-scale crowdsourcing task. (2) Algorithm itself is complicated and impracticable for crowdsourcing tasks involving creativity.

3   Overview of PDCCP

In this Crowdsourcing Platform for Professional Dictionary Compilation (PDCCP), the crowdsourcing task is compiling a cloud-computing dictionary. We extracted cloud computing related words and phrases from large amount of references and composed a cloud computing words database. Next, we create a crowdsourcing online translation platform, and let every Internet user who can visit the online translation web to attend this crowdsourcing task.

Due to the data in words database are all professional terms of cloud computing, or even the most recent artificial words, abbreviations and phrases appeared in references, translation work and translation result examine are all hard for computer to automatically complete. At the same time, every word or phrase's translation task is a subtask of compiling the cloud computing dictionary and one task attendant can only finish part of the compiling work. Thus, this is a typical "collaboration crowdsourcing task" and its suitable to apply the "large-scale automatic non-computer testing method".

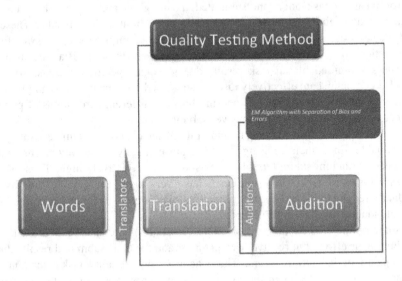

Fig. 1. Overview Structure of PDCCP

As showed in the Fig.1, the basic crowdsourcing task is translation. Translators as task attendants get words from database and submit their translation results online. The interesting part of PDCCP is that we used another crowdsourcing task for the quality testing method part of translation results. The auditors with the translation results as their subtasks submit their judgments as audition results online. Then we applied Expectation Maximization Algorithm with Separation of Bias and Errors to control the quality of auditions. The final audition results serve as a feedback of translators work quality. If the words pass it will be in the professional dictionary, otherwise it will give back to the translators to redo the translation.

The relationship of these two crowdsourcing tasks is that the auditor's crowdsourcing task works as the non-computing automatic testing method for quality control of translators' crowdsourcing task. This also provides a dynamic working mode that can apply different task distribution strategies to stimulate task efficiency and quality.

4   Quality Testing Method in PDCCP

For creative crowdsourcing tasks, computer might not be able to complete task quality testing or the cost will be too high. In this situation, human testing must be applied. However, due to the large-scale of most crowdsourcing tasks, the cost of human testing is hard to control and the efficiency often does not satisfy the company's expectation. There is no effective solution for this problem at the present. The following are crowdsourcing quality testings' two features: (1) the scale of task is large, (2) it need human to finish the testing. These two features quite match crowdsourcing characteristics. Through some appropriate changes, we can make crowdsourcing task A's quality testing as crowdsourcing task B. Then we can achieve crowdsourcing A's quality testing by accomplishing crowdsourcing task B.

How to make crowdsourcing task A's quality testing as crowdsourcing task B's subtasks is the key of this method. At the same time, crowdsourcing task B should have an existing method to finish the quality testing for itself. To design crowdsourcing task B as a "multilevel label judgment" type of the crowdsourcing task is a good choice. No matter crowdsourcing task A is independent crowdsourcing task or collaborating crowdsourcing task, the method we mentioned above is convenient to achieve. For example, crowdsourcing task A is professional terms translation, and crowdsourcing task B is translation quality judgment. The need to review the quality of crowdsourcing task A's submitted results forms the crowdsourcing task B. Since these are only simple judgments for human, we can apply Gold Standard Test or the Expectation-Maximization Algorithm with Separation of Bias and Errors. Thus, conveniently obtained the crowdsourcing task A's quality testing result.

4.1 Process

In Fig. 2, the meanings of abbreviations are: TASA (Task Attendants Set of crowdsourcing task A), TASB (Task Attendants Set of crowdsourcing task B), SSA (Subtasks of crowdsourcing task A), SSB (Subtasks of crowdsourcing task B).

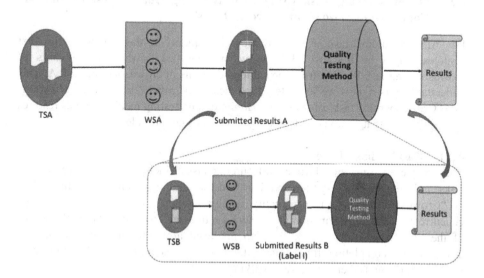

Fig. 2. Process of Quality Testing Method

The explanation of the process:

1. One task attendant of crowdsourcing task A ($taa \in TASA$) submitted a subtask of crowdsourcing task A ($sa \in SSA$) and produced a *Submit(taa, sa)*.

2. For *Submit(taa, sa)* form a corresponding quality testing subtask *sb* and put into *SSB*.

3. One task attendant of crowdsourcing task B ($tab \in TASB$) submitted a subtask of crowdsourcing task B ($sb \in SSB$) and produced a *Submit(tab, sb)* or called label *l[tab][sb]*.

4. Update label and get the new label *l* using Expectation Maximization Algorithm with Separation of Bias and Errors. Then we can obtain the correct label *T(sb)* for every subtasks of crowdsourcing task B and *Cost(sb)* for the recoverable bias cost of every task attendants in crowdsourcing task B.

5. From the correct label *T(sb)* we can educe the corresponding quality or grade of *Submit(taa, sa)* then get the quality evaluation of every task attendants of crowdsourcing task A.

Generally, TASA and TASB have no intersection mainly due to the following two considerations: (1) Task attendants only focused on one single work, will be practiced in it soon and the cost of training is relatively low. (2) Task attendants that concurrently involved in both tasks might be self-deceptive to judge their own results.

4.2 "Crowdsourcing Task Using Crowdsourcing Quality Testing Method" Compared to "Two Crowdsourcing Tasks"

For "Crowdsourcing task using crowdsourcing quality testing method", the first response might be it's just "Two crowdsourcing tasks" while the subtasks of crowdsourcing task B come from the submitted results of crowdsourcing task A. This understanding is right if we separately look these two crowdsourcing tasks. However, as a "Crowdsourcing task using crowdsourcing quality testing method", it has features and advantages that "Two crowdsourcing tasks" does not provide.

4.2.1 Task's Finish Time

The completion time of "Two crowdsourcing tasks" includes two crowdsourcing tasks' independent working time and their transformation and generation time. While in "Crowdsourcing task using quality testing method", two tasks are working concurrently. The transformation and generation time are covered in the working time of the two crowdsourcing tasks and do not need any extra time consummation. Therefore its completion time equals the two crowdsourcing tasks' independent working time minus their concurrent working time.

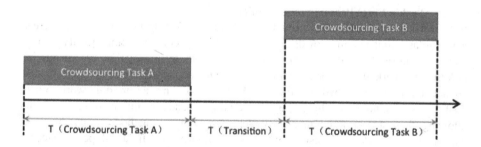

Fig. 3. Two Crowdsourcing Tasks Timeline

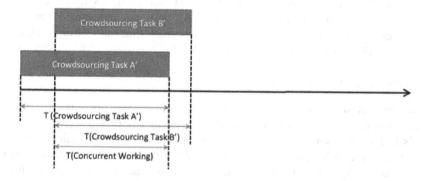

Fig. 4. Crowdsourcing Task using Quality Testing Method Timeline

In Fig.3, we see: T(two crowdsourcing tasks) = T(crowdsourcing task A) + T(transition)+ T(crowdsourcing task B)

In Fig.4, we see: T(crowdsourcing task using quality testing method) = T(crowdsourcing task A') + T(crowdsourcing task B') – T(concurrent working)

In above equations:

a) Generally, crowdsourcing task B' started soon after crowdsourcing task A' began or they start at the same time. Thus T(concurrent working) ≈ T(crowdsourcing task A') then T(crowdsourcing task using crowdsourcing quality testing method) ≈ T(crowdsourcing task B').

b) Since during the process of crowdsourcing task A' we can get quality feedback of its submitted results, we can promote valid submitted results with the assistance of effective crowdsourcing task mode. Therefore, normally T(crowdsourcing task A') is slightly smaller than T(crowdsourcing task A).

c) Compared to crowdsourcing task B, crowdsourcing task B' in its process might be influenced by the completion of crowdsourcing task A. Thus T(crowdsourcing task B') is usually greater than T(crowdsourcing task B).

d) By technical methods, T(transition) might be controlled to lower level.

For tasks' finish time, the following are advantages of "Crowdsourcing task using quality testing method": (1) two crowdsourcing tasks work concurrently and saves large amount of task time. (2) It does not need form and transition time.

4.2.2   Task's Final Performance Quality

In "Crowdsourcing task using crowdsourcing quality testing method", when there is new subtask finished in crowdsourcing task B, the corresponding quality control feedback can send to crowdsourcing task A. Using these information, crowdsourcing task A can work under corresponding mode and adjust strategies to identify task attendant's quality in crowdsourcing task A, distributing more important work to high quality task attendant while giving low quality attendants minor subtasks or not allowing them to work anymore. By deploying similar methods, companies can enhance the submitted task results and indirectly improve the final task performance.

This closed loop feedback working mode is the advantage that two independent crowdsourcing tasks cannot achieve. Since in two independent crowdsourcing tasks crowdsourcing task B starts after crowdsourcing task A finished, the low quality submitted results in crowdsourcing task A will be maintained and bring crowdsourcing task B some nonsense work costing time and efforts. This is a fundamental distinction of these two concepts.

4.3   Dynamic Working Mode

In dynamic working mode, to certain task attendants, their task distribution is affected by the submitted results' quality of other task attendants or themselves. The next stage's task distribution has uncertainty. Task attendants have interactions, might be competence or collaboration. Compared to static working mode, dynamic working mode's superiority is it can take advantage of the feedback of submitted results. By integrating the dynamic working mode with appropriate quality testing method, we can get real-time quality feedback of submitted results and task attendants. This also fits the quality testing method we mentioned above.

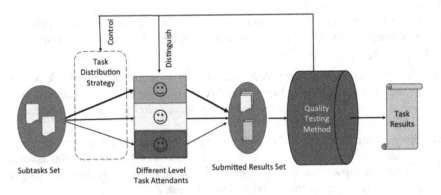

Fig. 5. Dynamic Working Mode

As showed in Fig. 5, the feedback of quality testing method distinguishes task attendants with different quality levels and results in different task distribution strategies.

1) Improve Submitted Task Quality

After getting various task attendants' quality testing feedback, we can use strategies and distinguish them. In normal situation, we intend to give the higher quality, more activated and more experienced task attendant the more important subtask; vice versa. According to different task attendants' conditions, we can collect task attendants' submitted task results quality and all tasks' frequency and operation time to obtain some reflections.

2) Improve Task Efficiency

In Dynamic working mode, we can use all task attendants' information and design different stimulating methods and competing system. These methods can keep updating or by combining several methods to achieve better effects.

3) Problems

To enhance all functions mentioned above, we need to complete a large number of calculations. As crowdsourcing task, the data in itself is big already; and this becomes an obstacle on the way. Zhang Zhiqiang [6] proposed a compatible solution that to change the real time crowdsourcing quality testing feedback adjustment to periodic crowdsourcing quality testing feedback adjustment. This not only can relieve the problem of large amount of calculations, but also ensures company can get crowdsourcing quality feedback and achieve closed loop quality control.

This quality testing method provides a solution to solve large-scale non-computing automatic testing, increases adaptability for the content of crowdsourcing tasks and suits crowdsourcing tasks that related to groups or sociality. The disadvantages of this quality testing method are the algorithm itself is complicated and it consists of a large amount of human factors might make tasks have relatively high uncertainty.

5   Task Distribution Strategy in PDCCP

For task distribution strategy, there hasn't been systematical analysis and research. In PDCCP, we have tried two task distribution strategy.

5.1   Static Strategy

This strategy is under static working mode. Task attendants get fixed number of subtask each time and the system update new subtasks only after all old subtasks are done.

5.2   Competency Strategy

Competency strategy is a dynamic task distribution strategy that considers task attendant's enthusiasm, quality and quantity of submitted results among all task attendant. Each time, task attendants choose to finish one subtask from a set of subtasks, and system updated subtasks set before task attendant start to choose next subtask. Generally, task attendants intend to choose the easiest one from the subtasks set.

After some time, the difficulty of the rest of the subtasks will increase. Thus, the earlier task attendants finish their task, the easier subtasks they can choose to complete. This competency stimulates the finish time of crowdsourcing task and increasese efficiency. At the same time, the more subtasks provided each time, the easier subtask task attendatns can choose from. Making relations between the amount of subtasks in the set task attendant can choose from with task attendant's motivation and quality and quantity of submitted results among all task attendants can monitor task attendants and enhance task quality.

6   Experiments and Result Analysis

The main purpose of crowdsourcing platform for professional dictionary compilation is to implement basic functions of online translation and audition, including words distribution, translation results submission and audition, and audition results submission. In PDCCP, every user can register login and logout but we strictly divide the permission of different types of users. For translators they can only get words list and submit translation result while for auditors they can only judge translation results and submit feedback. For admins, they can see the statistics in management and monitor the process of crowdsourcing task.

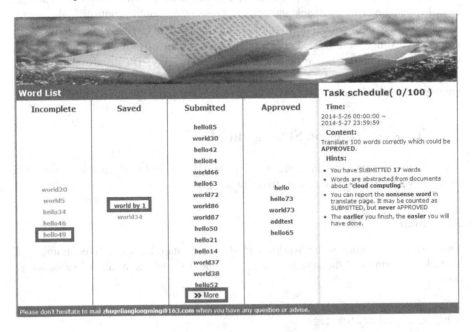

Fig. 6. Translator's interface

As showed in above Fig. 6, translators can choose the words from Incomplete column and do the translation. They can either save the word for further edition, as appeared in Saved column, or they can submit it then the words will appear in

Submitted column. Once the word is submitted, it will be marked as ready for audition and distribute to auditor's interface, which showed in the above Fig. 7. Translators cannot edit the translation of their submitted words unless the auditors evaluate it as a Bad Result and the system give the word back to translator's Saved list. If the word passed audition, meanning that auditors judged it as a good result, it will be regard as a good translation that could be add to the professional dictionary.

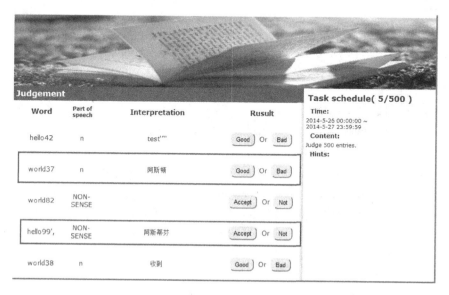

Fig. 7. Auditor's interface

This PDCCP is based on MVC (Model-View-Controller) framework, using the currently popular method that separates the logic, interface and database to organize the code. The Controller is responsible for reading the data from View and sending data requirement or command to Model according to the logic. The Model is responsible for access data or other operations from data port. The View is responsible for the results display after data processing and it's the most important class for user interaction. The View receives the data processed by the Controller and displays after self-processing. The following Fig. 14 is only a simplified class diagram for PDCCP; in fact the real class diagram is more substantial and complicated.

Besides the introduction of PDCCP, as we mentioned in early sections, for this large-scale non-computing automatic testing crowdsourcing task type, we proposed a Quality Control Method in PDCCP and also explored some Distribution Strategy in PDCCP. In the following paragraphs, we will focus on the quality and efficiency influences of Quality Control Method and Task Distribution Strategy in PDCCP.

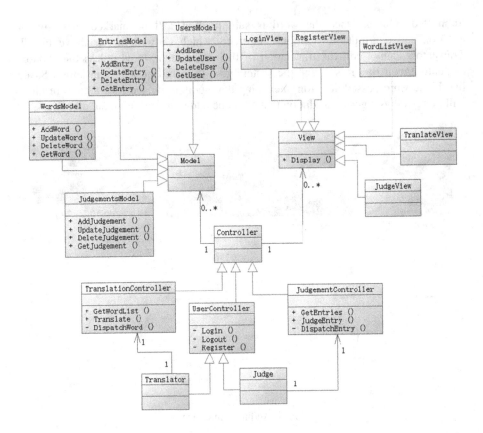

6.1   Efficiency Influence of Quality Testing Method in PDCCP

To determine the efficiency influences of *Quality Testing Method in PDCCP*, we randomly picked 560 words from database twice for the first and second crowdsourcing experiments. The translators in these two experiments are all first time doing translation. The differences between these two are in the first experiment, auditors begin the audition after all translators finished their job; while in the second experiment, auditors start the audition soon after the translators began their translations. In these experiment, we used static distribution, giving translators 10 subtasks each time and updating 10 new words after the translator finished all former 10 words.

In these two experiments, we start time calculation after the first translation submitted, and update the amount of finished subtasks per hour. In the following figure, the blue means translators' workload and the red indicates auditors' workload.

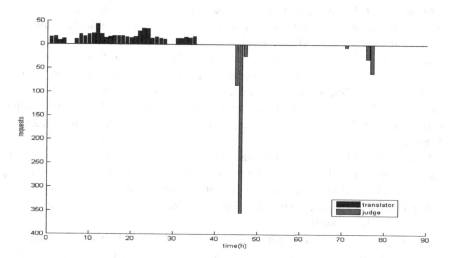

Fig. 8. Two independent crowdsourcing tasks

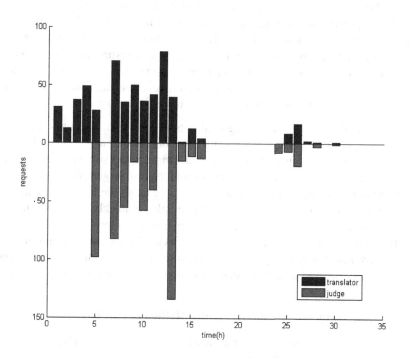

Fig. 9. Crowdsourcing task using quality control method

As showed in Fig. 8, auditors audition begins after the translation all finished. In this task, translators cost 124343s and auditors cost 115010s to finish their work. The transition time is 37153s and the total time is 276506s. T(two crowdsourcing tasks) = T(translation) + T(transition)+ T(audition) = 124343s+37153s+115010s = 276506s.

In this process, we need to point out that there are obvious two parts of audition. The first part's efficiency is pretty high but the second part lagged to begin and procrastinate the total task time. If the second part of audition can begin earlier, which means to reduce the audition cost to 5156s, then the total task time might reduce to 166661s.

As showed in Fig. 9, audition began soon after the translation had started. In this task, translators cost 104882s and auditors cost 91671s and their concurrent working time is 90467s. The total time cost is 106086s. T(crowdsourcing task using quality testing method) = T(translation) + T(audition) – T(concurrent working) = 104882s + 91671s – 90467s = 106086s

In this process, auditors' work a little lagged behind translators' work. And auditions are separate to two parts due to the translators are not promptly finish their work.

With the data above, we can conclude that the efficiency of crowdsourcing task using quality testing method is 276506s/106086s=2.61 times of the efficiency of two crowdsourcing tasks. At the same time, if auditors finished their work in time in two crowdsourcing tasks, its audition efficiency is 90467s/5165s=15.52 times of the audition efficiency in crowdsourcing task using quality testing method. In addition, for every word, translators spend much more time than auditors. The average translation time is 43s, but the average audition time is less than 5s. For the pros and cons of these two experiments, we have the following summary:

(1) For crowdsourcing task using quality testing method, audition started earlier and finished earlier. However, the span of the total audition time is longer. Due to some other factors, such as translators worked too slowly, the efficiency of the task might decrease and the task stagnated.

(2) Oppositely, for two crowdsourcing tasks, if under the highest efficiency and highest rate of work, task might be completed quickly. However, if sudden events happened, its ability to handle emergency is low.

(3) Therefore, we suggest quality testing method for crowdsourcing tasks that have lower audition speed. For crowdsourcing tasks with fast audition speed, not considering quality feedback, we might use two crowdsourcing tasks.

6.2   Quality Influence of Quality Testing Method in PDCCP

In this experiment, we didn't prepare corresponding ground truth. Therefore, we used human auditing the quality after the experiment.

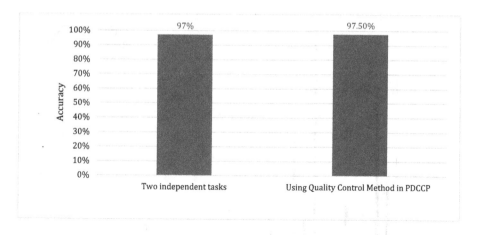

Fig. 10. Accuracy Comparison

The above data in Fig.10 shows that the accuracy of crowdsourcing task using quality control method is 97.5% while the two crowdsourcing tasks got 97% accuracy.

Thus, the quality control method does not have direct influences on the task quality and might due to following reasons: (1) With static distribution strategy, we didn't make use of the feedback of quality control method. (2) In this experiment, task attendants are all college students that have some knowledge of cloud computing, thus the average quality is too high to show whether quality control method affects the task quality or not.

6.3 Efficiency Influence of Task Distribution Strategy in PDCCP

As we mentioned in previous section, we tried static strategy and competency strategy for this experiment. The static strategy give fixed number of words to task attendants each time and only updated the new words after the former words are all done. The competency strategy gives task attendants opportunities to choose the easiest words from a set of words every time. The earlier they finish the easier words they may choose from, thus created a competency between task attendants.

As before, we randomly picked 560 words from database twice for the static and competency strategy experiments. Task attendants are the same for these two experiments. In these two experiments, we start calculating time after the first translation submitted, and update the amount of finished subtasks per hour. In the following figure, the red means translators' work performance using static strategy and the blue indicates translators' work performance with competency strategy.

In the above Fig. 11, task attendants under competency strategy worked mostly during the beginning of the task time while task attendants' work performance distributing evenly under static strategy. Thus demonstrated the efficiency advantage of competency strategy. To analysis the efficiency more clearly, we use the calculative work performance in the following figure. The green line shows the task

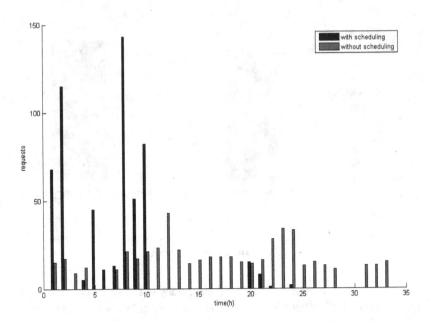

Fig. 11. Task attendants' work performance under static and competency strategy

attendants' accumulative work performance under static strategy, while the blue curve shows the task attendants' accumulative work performance under competency strategy.

As in Fig. 12, started from the beginning, the accumulative performance of translators under competency strategy is always higher than the accumulative performance of translators under static strategy. Therefore, the competency task distribution strategy stimulated task attendants to finish the task earlier.

By statistics, the completion time of static strategy is 124343s and the average subtask completion time is 62388.15s; while the completion time of competency strategy is 84940s. The efficiency of it is 124343s/84940s = 1.46 times of the efficiency under static strategy. The average subtask completion time is 21956.44s, and its efficiency is 62388.15s/21956.44s =2.84 times of the efficiency under static strategy.

In addition, in Fig. 12, in both experiments there exists a period of lagging time. It might due to the task attendants are not active or they might missed the advantageous time of the competency strategy and lack motivation.

In future experiments, we should pay attention to the potential of task distribution strategy improvement since different task distribution strategy does have great impact on the efficiency.

6.4   Quality Influence of Task Distribution Strategy in PDCCP

In this experiment, we didn't prepare corresponding ground truth. Therefore, we used human auditing the quality after the experiment.

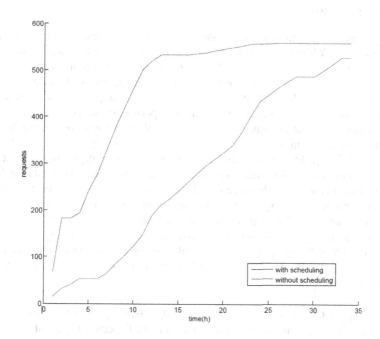

Fig. 12. Translators' accumulative work performance under static and competency strategy

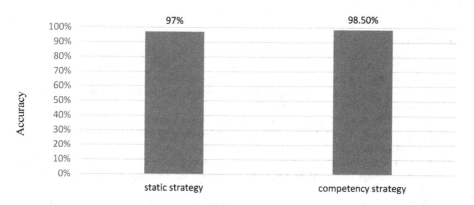

Fig. 13. Accuracy Comparison

As the audition results showed in Fig. 13, the accuracy of crowdsourcing task using static strategy is 97% and crowdsourcing task using competency strategy's accuracy is 98.5%.

In this experiment, task distribution method does have some influences on the quality of crowdsourcing task but not quite noteworthy. The reason might be task attendants are all college students that have some knowledge of cloud computing, thus the average quality is too high to show whether quality control method affects the task quality or not.

7   Conclusion

In this paper, we introduced a large-scale non-computing automatic testing crowdsourcing task for professional dictionary compilation (PDCCP) and mainly focused on the quality control method in it. We proposed a quality testing method that uses another crowdsourcing task for the quality testing (audition) part of translation task. We also explored some task distribution strategy, static or competency, to stimulate task attendants to finish their work earlier. From the experiments, we concluded that quality testing method has great influences to efficiency while less impact on quality due to the ineffective task distribution strategy that should take advantage of quality feedbacks or the ensured high quality of task attendants. Competency strategy compared to static strategy has more remarkable effects on efficiency but it does not have notable influences on quality that might due to the overall high quality of task attendants. In the future, (1) we should increase the experiment size and complexity and further measure the influences of quality testing method and task distribution strategy to crowdsourcing task efficiency and quality. (2) We should improve task distribution strategy based on the feedback from quality testing method. (3) Explore other potential of crowdsourcing task, such as try to determine the difficulty level of subtasks and better the task distribution method to enhance efficiency.

Acknowledgement. This work is partially supported by China National Science Foundation (Granted Number 61272438, 61472253), Research Funds of Science and Technology Commission of Shanghai Municipality (Granted Number 14511107702, 12511502704).

References

[1] Howe, J.: The rise of crowdsourcing. Wired Magazine 14(6), 1–4 (2006)

[2] Brabham, D.C.: Crowdsourcing as a model for problem solving an introduction and cases. Convergence: The International Journal of Research into New Media Technologies 14(1), 75–90 (2008)

[3] Walter, S.D.: Gold Standard Test Encyclopedia of Biostatistics

[4] Dempster, A.P., Laird, N.M., Rubin, D.B.: Maximum likelihood from incomplete data via the EM algorithm. Journal of the Royal Statistical Society 39(1), 1–38 (1977)

[5] Ipeirotis, P.G., Provost, F., Wang, J.: Quality management on amazon mechanical turk. In: Proceedings of the ACM SIGKDD Workshop on Human Computation, pp. 64–67. ACM (2010)

[6] Zhang, Z., Pang, J., Xie, X.: Research on crowdsourcing strategy of quality control and evaluation algorithm. Chinese Journal of Computers 36(8), 1636–1649 (2013)

[7] Howe, J.: The rise of crowdsourcing. Wired Magazine 14(6), 1–4 (2006)

[8] Brabham, D.C.: Crowdsourcing as a model for problem solving an introduction and cases. Convergence: the International Journal of Research into New Media Technologies 14(1), 75–90 (2008)

[9] Doan, A., Ramakrishnan, R., Halevy, A.Y.: Crowdsourcing systems on the world-wide web. Communications of the ACM 54(4), 86–96 (2011)

[10] Franklin, M.J., Kossmann, D., Kraska, T., et al.: CrowdDB: answering queries with crowdsourcing. In: Proceedings of the 2011 ACM SIGMOD International Conference on Management of Data, pp. 61–72. ACM (2011)

HelpMe: A Heuristic License Plate Correction Method for Big Data Application

Guochao Jia, Xu Tao, Yan Liu, and Wanchun Dou*

State Key Laboratory for Novel Software Technology, Nanjing University
Nanjing, 210023, P.R.China
{jackjianju,wondertx,zizhuoy}@gmail.com
douwc@nju.edu.cn

Abstract. Serving as a critical feature of vehicle flow in Intelligent Transportation System (ITS) of Smart City, license plate information has been applied in many momentous transportation applications. However, ITS suffers from the low accuracy of license plate recognition due to changeful and uncontrollable environment and machinery malfunction from traffic equipment deployed on a large scale. Therefore, it is challenging for license plate recognition to satisfy high accuracy and low latency in the condition of large-scale traffic data sets. In this paper, a Heuristic License Plate Correction Method, named HelpMe, is proposed to address the challenges above. It aims at recognizing and correcting the incorrect license plate information in real-time with high accuracy. Technically, a heuristic method is adopted to guide the correction process. Moreover, in order to process the large-scale data sets efficiently, HelpMe is implemented on HANA cluster (an in-memory database). Finally, extensive experiments are conducted on a real-world data set to evaluate the feasibility and efficiency of HelpMe.

Keywords: Intelligent Transportation System, license plate recognition and correction, heuristic method, in-memory database, big data application

1 Introduction

Recent years have witnessed an explosive growth of traffic data which is collected by diversiform devices and sensors such as cameras, RFID tags, vehicle GPS trackers and so on. These large data sets, so-called "Big Data"[1,2], have a strong influence on both academia and industry. In order to cope with complex and changeable traffic situation, Smart City comes into being [3,4,5,6]. Currently, many Chinese cities have made a considerable development in the process of Smart City construction, especially in ITS [7,8]. Hundreds of Smart Base Stations (SBSs) have been built along the primary road in urban areas. The SBS is an advanced monitoring device equipped with HD cameras and sensitive RFID readers. Not all vehicles are equipped with RFID tags, especially non-local ones.

---

* Corresponding author.

J. Cao et al. (Eds.): PAS 2014, CCIS 495, pp. 93–107, 2015.
© Springer-Verlag Berlin Heidelberg 2015

ITS deploys SBSs to build a fundamental transportation monitoring network for real-time and quick-response traffic applications. A SBS could capture various kinds of vehicle information including license plate information. The challenge is that Automatic License Plate Recognition (ALPR) cannot satisfy accuracy requirements of ITS due to changeable weather and machinery malfunction among the large-scale deployment SBSs [9,10]. Moreover, it is hard for ALPR to get a quick response and high performance under the circumstances of real-time and large-scale traffic datasets.

In view of these challenges, a heuristic license plate correction method, named HelpMe, is presented in this paper to improve the accuracy of ALPR. Unlike ALPR, creative heuristic license plate inspection and correction algorithms are applied in HelpMe and are deployed on HANA cluster. Therefore, HelpMe obtains a real-time performance and high accuracy compared to ALPR.

The remainder of the paper is organized as follows: preliminary knowledge about our method is presented in Section 2. Then a heuristic license plate correction method, named HelpMe, is described in Section 3 in detail. In Section 4, experiments are designed and analyzed to evaluate the veracity and time consuming of HelpMe. Related works are presented in Section 5. Finally, the paper is concluded and an outlook on our future work is discussed in Section 6.

2   Preliminary Knowledge

In-Memory Database. An In-Memory database (IMDB) is a database management system that primarily relies on main physical memory for computer data storage compared with conventional database management systems (Disk Resident Database, DRDB) that employ a disk storage mechanism [11]. The key difference is that in IMDB the primary copy lives permanently in memory. As a consequence, IMDB can provide much better response times and transaction throughputs compared to DRDB [12]. In this paper, HelpMe is proposed to implement on high performance analytics appliance database platform (HANA) to meet the acquirement of real-time license plate correction [13]. The SAP HANA platform is a flexible data source agnostic in-memory data platform that allows users to analyze large volumes of data in real-time.

Automatic License Plate Recognition. Automatic license plate recognition (ALPR) is a mass surveillance method that uses optical character recognition on images to read vehicle registration plates [14,15]. Typically, ALPR is used in road-rule enforcement cameras or closed-circuit television, as a method of electronic toll collection on pay-per-use roads and cataloging the movements of traffic and individuals for various police forces. ALPR commonly uses infrared lighting to allow the camera to take the picture at any time of the day. Many primary algorithms implemented to identify a license plate from the images captured by the cameras. However, no one algorithm can guarantee the absolute accuracy. Existing systems have so many problems although lots of improvements in image recognition have been made to decrease error rate [16,17].

3   A Heuristic License Plate Correction Method(HelpMe)

In this paper, a heuristic license plate correction method, named HelpMe, is proposed for improving accuracy of ALPR for urban transportation infrastructure monitoring network. In this method, a heuristic algorithm is applied for license plate correctness inspection. And a character transition probability table (CTPT) is built through data fusion which is used for prediction of license plate correction. HelpMe aims to distinguish correctly captured license plates from those might be incorrect. And for the incorrect license plates, their corresponding potentially correct license plates are aggregated from the camera's neighborhoods attempting to fix the incorrect ones.

Table 1. Notational and symbolic conventions

Symbol	Description
LP	The license plate
TLP	The plates which are deemed to be trustworthy
SLP	The plates which are deemed to be suspicious
CLP	The plates which are corrected
CA	The camera set, $CA = \{ca_1, ca_2, ..., ca_n\}$
p_i	The precision of the camera $ca_i \in CA$
$Pr(LP)$	The probability that plate LP is correctly recognized
$Nb_k(ca_i)$	k degree neighbors of the camera $ca_i \in CA$

3.1   A Motivated Example

In this section, we fist provide an intuitive description of our method. Afterwards, several formal definitions are provided in the following with some probability theory to guarantee the reliability of our proposed method. Table 1 summarizes the symbols and notations used in this paper.

Firstly, for an individual vehicle, suppose that there is a road along which there are n cameras $CA = \{ca_1, ca_2, ..., ca_n\}$ and the vehicle will run through the road. In this situation, every camera will take a photo for the vehicle when it passes by a certain position. As a result, there will be n pictures associated

Fig. 1. A vehicle crosses cameras CA

with the car, when it runs through the road. Here, let Pic_Set stand for the set of the pictures, i.e., $Pic\_Set = \{pic_1, pic_2, ..., pic_n\}$.

For a picture pic_i, $pic_i \in Pic\_Set$, it contains the information of the vehicle's license plate. Let LPD indicate the real character string appearing on the vehicle's license plate. Let lpd_i indicate the character string of the vehicle's license plate extracted from the picture pic_i. For the n pictures contained in Pic_Set, n character strings could be extracted from the pictures. Here, let LP_Set indicate the set of n character strings, i.e., $LP\_Set = \{lpd_1, lpd_2, ..., lpd_n\}$.

With these assumptions, two cases will be discussed here.

- For a lpd_i, if $lpd_i = LPD$, we believe that the camera ca_i captures the right information appearing on the vehicle's license plate.
- For a lpd_i, if $lpd_i \neq LPD$, we believe that the camera ca_i did not capture the right information appearing on the car's license plate.

Furthermore, if we could not get the LPD in advance, an assumption as defined by Def. 1 is presented here for get the right information of the car's license plate.

Definition 1. *For a lpd_i, $lpd_i \in LP\_Set$, $LP\_Set = \{lpd_1, lpd_2, ..., lpd_n\}$, if there are m other elements contained in Pic_Set, which have the same data with lpd_i, the probability of lpd_i captured by the cameras along the road could be computed by $(m+1)/n$. For a lpd_i, if it owns the maximum probability value, it will be treated as the right information of the license plate.*

Def. 1 is enabled by an assumption that it is a small probability event for the cameras along the road to make same mistake.

In this paper, we assume that all cars on roads are not stationary but floating. Since two adjacent cameras stand only a few kilometers apart in the urban areas, this assumption assures us that floating cars inevitably come across several cameras and thereby get captured by them. As to cars which are captured only once by a camera and then disappeared from the neighboring camera, we deem it as an exception since this situation is rather rare.

Several formal definitions are given in the following to support our method in detail.

Definition 2 (A Trustworthy License Plate, TLP).

TLPs are those plates that are needless to correct. Given a set of cameras $CA = \{ca_1, ca_2, ..., ca_n\}$, if a vehicle goes through all the cameras in CA and is captured as the same plate LP, as depicted in Fig. 1, we claim that LP is a correctly recognized plate whose probability can be lower bounded by

$$Pr(LP) \geq 1 - p_i \prod_{j=1}^{n} (1 - p_j) \tag{1}$$

Here, p_i indicates the precision of the camera $ca_i \in CA$.

Definition 3 (A Suspicious License Plate, SLP).
A license plate LP is deemed to be suspicious if it only occurs in a single camera ca_i and does not emerge in its $n-1$ neighbors $CA' = \{ca_1, ca_2, ..., ca_{n-1}\}$. Otherwise, it should be captured by the neighboring cameras of ca_i with high probability. We claim that LP is a suspicious plate, and the probability that it is incorrectly recognized can also be lower bounded by:

$$Pr(SLP) \geq 1 - p_i \prod_{j=1}^{n-1}(1 - p_j) \tag{2}$$

Here, p_i indicates the precision of the camera $ca_i \in CA'$.

Definition 4 (k-degree Neighbors of a Camera).
The vast cameras deployed all over the city can be modeled as a directed graph $G = \{V, E\}$, here $V = CA$ is the set of all cameras, and E denotes the road between cameras. For any two cameras ca_i, ca_j, and $ca_i, ca_j \in V$, if ca_i is connected to ca_j directly by roads without crossing another ca_k, $\langle ca_i, ca_j \rangle \in E$. For a ca_i, its k-degree neighbors are those cameras from which it takes k hops to camera ca_i, plus those cameras to which it takes k hops from camera ca_i. Especially, 0-degree stands for current camera itself. Formally, k-degree neighbors $Nb_k(ca_i)$ of camera ca_i can be defined as follows:

$$Nb_k(ca_i) = \begin{cases} \{ca_j| < ca_i, ca_j >\in E \vee < ca_j, ca_i >\in E\}, & k = 1 \\ \{ca_j| (< ca_k, ca_j >\in E \vee < ca_j, ca_k >\in E) \wedge ca_k \in Nb_{k-1}(ca_i)\}, & k > 1 \end{cases} \tag{3}$$

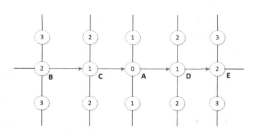

Fig. 2. k-degree neighbors of node A

Fig. 2 is an abstract view of roads and cameras in urban area. In Fig. 2, the nodes stand for cameras and the links stand for roads. The number k in nodes stands for k-degree of node A. For example, there are 4, 6, 4 points corresponding to 1,2,3-degree neighbors respectively.

3.2   A Heuristic License Plate Correction Method

A Heuristic License Plate Correction Method Framework. As a formal specification of the method has been introduced at the beginning of Section 3, an overview of HelpMe framework is depicted in Fig. 3.

In the framework, huge amount of RFID and ALPR detection results are original input of this method. There are four steps in HelpMe framework. Firstly, $TLPs$ Extraction, $TLPs$ would be extracted from the filtered ALPR detection results. Secondly, CTPT (Character Transition Probability Table) Generation, CTPT which generated through the data fusion of RFID and ALPR is used for predicting potential correct characters. Thirdly, $SLPs$ Correction, $SLPs$ would be corrected by Naïve Bayes theorem. Finally, $CLPs$ Accuracy Promotion, the accuracy of $CLPs$ would be improved by using RFID detection results through data fusion. And the optimization on image recognition is not the focus of this paper.

Detailed LP data classification and marking is shown in Fig. 4. Generally, LPs are classified into three levels during the process of HelpMe. Original LP data is the first level. $TLPs$ and $SLPs$ which belong to second level are marked by $TLPs$ Extraction. The results of $SLPs$ Correction which contains $CLPs$ and EXP (Exceptions) are regarded as the third level. EXP can be categorized to several types. For example, a vehicle crosses a single camera but stops for a long time which contradicts with the assumption of floating car. And the traffic is so sparse that little information can be extracted from a camera's neighbors.

Both $TLPs$ and $CLPs$ would be further corrected by RFID data fusion algorithm during the process of $CLPs$ Accuracy Promotion.

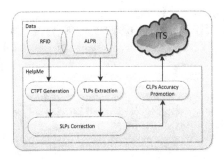 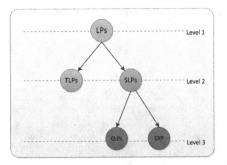

Fig. 3. Overview of the framework of HelpMe

Fig. 4. All possible cases of the execution of HelpMe

A more particular description of the process of HelpMe will be discussed in the following steps listed below.

$TLPs$ Extraction. The process of $TLPs$ Extraction aims to identify license plates that are correctly recognized with high probability. ALPR results are filtered through certain rules to clean the dirty data, such as overexposing pictures and files corrupted, etc. Distinguishing $TLPs$ from big traffic data poses a challenge to real time decision support. Therefore, we reduce the problem complexity by setting the limit on k of k-degree neighbors, the number θ of continuous occurrence when k is fixed ($\theta \leq 2k + 1$) and the travel interval Δt among CA.

Suppose the number of real occurrence of LP appeared in its 0,1,2,...,k-degree neighbors is θ', when $\theta' \geq \theta$ in its 0,1,2,...,k-degree neighbors in interval Δt, LP would be marked as TLP. Algorithm 1, $TPLs$ Extraction, illustrates the procedures of how $TLPs$ can be identified.

Algorithm 1. $TLPs$ Extraction

Input: The camera set CA, the limit of k when searching k-degree neighbors, the continuous occurrence limit θ, and the interval Δt between the camera in question and the k-degree neighbors

Output: The $TLPs$ of each camera $ca \in CA$

1: **for** each $ca \in CA$ **do**
2: **for** each LP recognized by ca **do**
3:   **if** $\theta' \geq \theta$ in its 0,1,2,...,k-degree neighbors in interval Δt **then**
4:    Mark LP as TLP;
5:   **end if**
6: **end for**
7: **end for**
8: **return** $TLPs$

Algorithm 1 checks whether θ can be satisfied first (line 3), if that does at some $k_i < k$, $TLPs$ Extraction only does calculate camera $ca's$ $k_i + 1, k_i + 2, ..., k$ degree neighbors. Thus it considerably deceases the time complexity of Algorithm 1. Assume that each camera has m 1-deree neighbors, if we do not set the constraint on θ, the time complexity of Algorithm 1 will be $O\left(nm^k\right)$. Now under the constraint of θ, Algorithm 1 breaks the inner loop whenever θ is met. Here Δt is used to filter out vehicles that are not the same as the LP in question, based on the assumption that vehicles are floating on the roads.

CTPT Generation (Character Transition Probability Table Generation). The purpose of the process of CTPT Generation is to generate character transition probability table which is applied for correcting $SLPs$. As pointed out in the beginning of Section 3, we think of the plate as a string. Most ALPR algorithms recognize each character of the plate independently.

Here, let $Char\_Set$ stand for the set of all characters recognized by ALPR, i.e., $Char\_Set = \{char_1, char_2, ..., char_n\}$. We can claim that for an incorrect plate recognized by ALPR, the position of the misrecognized character does not depend on other characters being correctly recognized or not. For each camera, a CTPT is built for predicting the error pattern.

Assume that each camera ca_i makes mistakes in its own way, $ca_i \in CA$, and there are many external factors affecting recognition result, such as weather conditions, light intensity, etc. Let $Weather\_Set = \{w_1, w_2, ..., w_n\}$ stand for variety of weather conditions, such as sunny, rainy, foggy, etc. Due to light intensity changes over time, we divide a day into six time periods for every four hours, i.e., $Time\_Set = \{t_1, t_2, t_3, t_4, t_5, t_6\}$. And to LPs taken by ca_i, $N\left(char_i|w, t\right)$

stands for all the number of character $char_i$ occurance appeared on LPs under weather w in the time period of t. Since RFID detector are accurate to be convincible, $N(char_i|w,t)$ would be generated according to RFID detector results. Accordingly, $N(char_i \to char_j|w,t)$ stands for the number of that character $char_i$ transforms into $char_j$ occurance recognized by ALPR under weather w in the time period of t.

Then given character $char_i$ and $char_j$, respectively stand for real character and recognized character at the same position in a LP, $char_i, char_j \in Char\_Set$. And $w \in Weather\_Set, t \in Time\_Set$, let

$$f(char_i, char_j, w, t) = \frac{N(char_i \to char_j|w,t)}{N(char_i)} \tag{4}$$

Here, $N(char_i)$ stands for all the number of character $char_i$ occurance appeared on the LP taken by ca_i. Formula (4) means that the character transition probability of $char_i$ transforms into $char_j$ under weather w in the time period of t.

CTPT is a table which has five columns including real character, recognized character, weather, time period and transition probability. By Formula (4), we can generate a CTPT for every ca_i, $ca_i \in CA$ for all weather conditions and time periods. CTPT would be updated in a certain period σ, and in this paper, we set σ as one week temporarily. In the further research, σ would be discussed in detail.

SLPs Correction. After Algorithm 1 is finished, most of correctly recognized plates have been identified. For those plates that are not marked as TLP in Algorithm 1, we deem them as $SLPs$. A SLP is not definitely an incorrectly recognized plate, just because the high probability it has. However, if this SLP is indeed incorrectly recognized, its corresponding correct plate should occur in its k-degree neighbors multiple times for some k.

Now, we define the similarity comparing LP to other LPs. Suppose there are n characters in LP and $char_i(LP)$ stands for the ith character of LP. The similarity of LP and LP' recognized by camera ca is described as follows:

$$sim(LP, LP') = \prod_{i=1}^{n} P(char_i(LP) \to char_i(LP')|w,t) \tag{5}$$

Here, $P(char_i(LP) \to char_i(LP')|w,t)$ stands for the probability of the ith character of LP transforms into the ith character of LP' under the weather w in the time period t. According to Nave Bayes theory [18],

$$sim(LP, LP') = \frac{\prod_{i=1}^{n} CTPT_{ca}(char_i(LP'), char_i(LP), w, t) * N(char_i(LP')|w,t)}{N(char_i(LP)|w,t)} \tag{6}$$

Here, $CTPT_{ca}\left(char_i\left(LP'\right), char_i\left(LP\right), w, t\right)$ stands for the CTPT value of camera ca under the condition of $char_i\left(LP'\right)$ which is the original character, $char_i\left(LP\right)$ which is $char_i\left(LP'\right)$ transformed into, weather w and time period t.

Based on this assumption, we propose a correction algorithm, namely $SLPs$ Correction, and there are two main steps including get potential $CLPs$ and correct $SLPs$. Basic steps are illustrated in Algorithm 2.

Algorithm 2. $SLPs$ Correction

Input: $SLPs$ of each camera $ca \in CA$, the limit of k when searching k-degree neighbors, the time t at which the SPL being captured, the continuous occurrence limit θ, and the interval Δt between the camera in question and the k-degree neighbors

Output: Output $CLPs$ for each camera $ca \in CA$ and its corresponding $SLPs$ in ca

1: **for** each $ca \in CA$ **do**
2:     // get potential CLPs
3:     $potentialCLPs = \varnothing$;
4:     **for** $i \leftarrow 1$ to k **do**
5:         **for** each LP recognized by ca **do**
6:             **if** $\theta' \geq \theta - 1$ in ca's 1,2,...,k-degree neighbors in interval Δt **then**
7:                 Add LP to $potentialCLPs$;
8:             **end if**
9:         **end for**
10:     **end for**
11:     //correct SLPs
12:     **for** each $slp \in SLPs$ **do**
13:         **if** $potentialCLPs$ equals $\varnothing$ **then**
14:             Mark slp as Exp;
15:         **else**
16:             Select most approximate slp' by maximizing $sim\left(slp, slp', w, t\right), slp' \in potentialCLPs$;
17:             Mark slp' as CLP;
18:         **end if**
19:     **end for**
20:     Output $CLPs$ and its corresponding $SLPs$;
21: **end for**

$CLPs$ Accuracy Promotion. To get a higher accuracy of $CLPs$, data fusion of RFID and ALPR is applied in the process of $CLPs$ Accuracy Promotion. Since RFID records are more accurate than ALPR to be convincible, those $CLPs$ whose original data both have ALPR LP records and RFID LP records could transform into the results recognized by RFID directly. In a way, promotion of $CLPs$ accuracy would be acquired to enhance the correction result. Algorithm 3, $CLPs$ Accuracy Promotion, shows the detail of how data fusion improves the $CLPs$ accuracy.

4   Experiment and Evaluation on In-Memory Database

In this section, experiments are designed to assess the veracity and time consuming of HelpMe. To evaluate the performance of HelpMe in veracity, ALPR

Algorithm 3. *CLPs* Accuracy Promotion

Input: *CLPs*, RFID data set
Output: *CLPs* with modified ones
1: **for** each *clp* ∈ *CLPs* **do**
2:     **if** *clp* has RFID record **then**
3:         **if** *clp* doesn't equal the *LP* of RFID information **then**
4:             *clp* ← *LP* of RFID information;
5:             Mark *clp* as modified;
6:         **end if**
7:     **end if**
8: **end for**
9: **return** *CLPs*;

---

is a control group in experiments. Five metrics are applied to evaluate the veracity: sensitivity, specificity, precision, accuracy and ROC (receiver operating characteristic) curve.

4.1 Experiment Data Sets and Evaluation Metrics

To evaluate the veracity and time consuming of HelpMe, real datasets are adopted in the experiments. Twenty representative SBSs in a primary road are selected to be experimental data source. And the data sets cover data collected during both day and night with different weather conditions. Data sets contain about 51,794,728 records of ALPR data and 33,971,265 records of RFID data ranging from Feb. 1st to Mar. 1st in Nanjing.

Sensitivity is referred to as the true positive (recognition) rate, while specificity is the true negative rate. In addition, precision is used to assess the percentage of tuples labeled as real that actually are real tuples. And accuracy is the combination of sensitivity and specificity. ROC curve is a useful visual tool for comparing binary classification model. A ROC curve shows the trade-off between sensitivity and specificity for a given model. The area under the ROC curve is a measure of the accuracy of the model.

4.2 Experiment Context

Technically, our experiments are conducted in a HANA cluster environment. The overview of the experiment context is depicted in Fig. 5, and the services recruited in our experiment are distributed among the cluster. And specific hardware and software configurations are as following:

- For hardware, the client is Lenovo Think-pad T430 machine with Intel i5-3210M 2.50 GHz processor, 4GB RAM and 250GB Hard Disk. And for master(one node) of HANA cluster is HP Z800 Workstation Intel(R) Multi-Core X5690 Xeon(R), 3.47GHz/12M Cache, 6 cores, 2 CPUs, 128GB DDR3 1066MHz ECC Reg RAM, 2TB 7.2K RPM SATA Hard Drive, for slave(one node) of HANA cluster is HP Z800 Workstation Intel(R) Multi-Core X5690 Xeon(R),

3.47GHz/12M Cache, 6 cores, 2 CPUs, 128GB DDR3 1066MHz ECC Reg RAM, 2TB 7.2K RPM SATA Hard Drive.
- For software, the client is equiped with Windows 7 Professional 64bit OS and the cluster installs HANA Studio and SUSE Enterprise Linux Server 11 SP3 with SAP HANA Platform SP07.

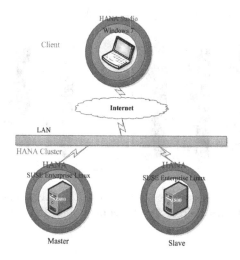

Fig. 5. The overview of experiment context

4.3   Experimental Evaluation

Two groups of experiments are conducted to measure the veracity and time consuming of HelpMe. In the first group, we compare HelpMe with ALPR in five aspects, sensitivity, specificity, precision, accuracy and ROC curve to evaluate the veracity of HelpMe. And in the second group, we explore the time consuming of HelpMe. And in all experiments, the value of k of $Nb_k(ca_i)$ is set to 2, 3, 4 respectively and $\theta = 3$ all the time.

Accuracy Evaluation. Metrics of sensitivity, specificity, precision, accuracy and ROC curve mainly indicate the veracity of HelpMe.

Comparison of HelpMe and ALPR in sensitivity, specificity, precision and accuracy. Sensitivity, specificity, precision and accuracy are four statistical measures of the performance of a binary classification test. The higher sensitivity, specificity, precision or accuracy represents the more accurate correction rate.

The sensitivity and specificity values of ALPR comparing with HelpMe with k value equals 2,3,4 are shown in Fig. 6. It could be found that the sensitivity and specificity values of HelpMe with k equals 2,3,4 are much higher than ALPR (e.g., the sensitivity values of HelpMe with k equals 2,3,4 are respectively 0.1943,

0.2847, 0.3004 higher than ALPR and the specificity values of HelpMe with k equals 2,3,4 are respectively 0.1875, 0.2352, 0.2813 higher than ALPR). Thus our method HelpMe can provide much higher hit rate than ALPR (0.2598 higher in sensitivity and 0.2347 higher in specificity averagely). And the larger k value is, more accurate the method is. But the growth of sensitivity and specificity becomes less obvious with the k value increases.

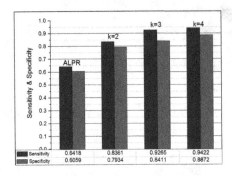 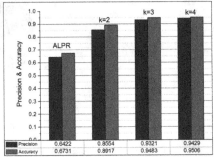

Fig. 6. Comparison of Sensitivity and Specificity of ALPR with HelpMe ($k=2$, 3, 4)

Fig. 7. Comparison of Precision and Accuracy of ALPR with HelpMe ($k=2$, 3, 4)

Fig. 7 shows the precision and accuracy values of ALPR comparing with HelpMe with k value equals 2, 3, 4. Obviously, the precision and accuracy of HelpMe are much higher than the traditional method ALPR. The precision of HelpMe with k value equals 2, 3, 4 are 0.2132, 0.2899, 0.3007 higher than ALPR respectively. To accuracy, HelpMe is 0.2571 higher than ALPR averagely. Besides, the change law of precision and accuracy of HelpMe is just like the sensitivity and specificity of HelpMe. With k increases, the precision and accuracy become higher but do not increase apparently like before.

Comparison of HelpMe and ALPR in ROC curve. ROC curve is an integrated indicator which reflects continuous variables of sensitivity and specificity. ROC curve reveals the relationship between sensitivity and specificity using the method of composition. The more area under the curve, the higher the prediction accuracy is. On the ROC curve, the coordinates of the point closest to the upper left of figure have both higher threshold of sensitivity and specificity.

The ROC curves of ALPR and HelpMe with k value equals 2, 3, 4 are presented in Fig. 8. Considering the area under the curve, HelpMe with k value equals 3 and 4 almost have the equivalent scale of area and the area of HelpMe with k value equals 4 is just a little larger than that with k value equals 3. Moreover, ALPR gets the smallest area. That is to say, ALPR has the lowest prediction accuracy. And considering the shape of all four ROC curves, the coordinates of points on HelpMe ROC curves are much closer to the upper left of the figure than ALPR. Consequently, HelpMe has higher sensitivity and specificity

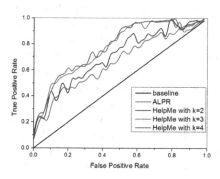 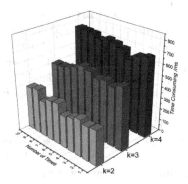

Fig. 8. ROC curves of ALPR and HelpMe (k=2, 3, 4)

Fig. 9. Time consuming of HelpMe (k=2, 3, 4)

than ALPR. And among ROC curves of HelpMe, HelpMe with k value equals 4 has the highest quality of veracity, and HelpMe with k value equals 3 is just a little inferior than that with k value equals 4.

All in all, HelpMe provides a better performance in veracity than ALPR. Thus our method would provide a higher veracity to satisfy the requirements of high level traffic applications in ITS.

Time Consuming Evaluation. Time consuming factor mainly indicates the efficiency of HelpMe.

The time consuming of HelpMe with k value equals 2, 3, 4 is shown in Fig. 9. Experiments with k equals 2, 3, 4 have been conducted 10 times respectively. As far as the scale of current data set, the higher k value of HelpMe, the time consuming becomes larger. It is easy to see that all cases with different k values are capable of meeting the requirements of upper applications of ITS. With consideration of all conditions, HelpMe with k equals 3 consumes less time than that with k equals 4 and has higher veracity than that with k equals 2. Therefore, HelpMe with k equals 3 is more comparable than those with other k values in this experiment.

Generally speaking, comparing with different k values, HelpMe has a stable time consuming. Moreover, HelpMe on HANA cluster has satisfactory performance on efficiency.

5   Related Works and Comparison Analysis

Most methods of license plate correction focus on ALPR algorithm optimization. And there have been many automatic license plate recognition (ALPR) methods developed in both academia and industry. In [9], the author shows that license plate algorithms in images or videos are generally composed of following three processing steps: 1) extraction of a license plate region; 2) segmentation of the plate characters; and 3) recognition of each character. In [10], a license plate recognition algorithm is proposed on the basis of a novel adaptive image segmentation technique and connected component analysis in conjunction with a character recognition neural network. They also describe various limitations of current license plate recognitions methods, and discuss possible extensions that can improve recognition capabilities and make automatic license plate recognition systems applicable to an even broader range of conditions.

To the best of our knowledge, compared with existing automatic license plate recognition methods, HelpMe further analysis the license plate from ALPR and correct the suspicious license plates to right ones, which makes ALPR more reliable. Moreover, HelpMe implemented on in-memory database has favorable scalability and efficiency, especially the real-time performance.

6   Conclusions and Future Work

In this paper, a heuristic license plate correction method, named HelpMe, is proposed for license plate correction. It can effectively correct the license plates which are wrongly recognized by ALPR. Algorithms proposed in HelpMe are achieved under HANA platform in order to get real-time response. Real-world data experiments indicate that our approach greatly improves the accuracy of ALPR, and can be employed to achieve real-time ITS applications.

In the future, we plan to enhance the robustness and applicability of HelpMe. For instance, applying more environment variable factors in HelpMe including but not limited to weather, lightness, average speed of vehicle, etc. And larger real-world data sets will be applied to impove our method. Moreover, real-world applications in ITS will further employ HelpMe to raise the accuracy and real-time performance of ALPR.

Acknowledgement. This paper is partly supported by the National Science Foundation of China under Grant No.91318301.

References

1. Manyika, J., Chui, M., Brown, B., Bughin, J., Dobbs, R., Roxburgh, C., Byers, A.H.: Big data: The next frontier for innovation, competition, and productivity (2011)
2. Mayer-Schönberger, V., Cukier, K.: Big data: A revolution that will transform how we live, work, and think. Houghton Mifflin Harcourt (2013)
3. Shapiro, J.M.: Smart cities: quality of life, productivity, and the growth effects of human capital. The Review of Economics and Statistics 88(2), 324–335 (2006)
4. Caragliu, A., Del Bo, C., Nijkamp, P.: Smart cities in europe. Journal of Urban Technology 18(2), 65–82 (2011)
5. Chourabi, H., Nam, T., Walker, S., Gil-Garcia, J.R., Mellouli, S., Nahon, K., Pardo, T.A., Scholl, H.J.: Understanding smart cities: An integrative framework. In: 2012 45th Hawaii International Conference on System Science (HICSS), pp. 2289–2297. IEEE (2012)

6. Schaffers, H., Komninos, N., Pallot, M., Trousse, B., Nilsson, M., Oliveira, A.: Smart cities and the future internet: Towards cooperation frameworks for open innovation. In: Domingue, J. (ed.) Future Internet Assembly, LNCS, vol. 6656, pp. 431–446. Springer, Heidelberg (2011)

7. Figueiredo, L., Jesus, I., Machado, J.T., Ferreira, J., de Carvalho, J.M.: Towards the development of intelligent transportation systems. Intelligent Transportation Systems 88, 1206–1211 (2001)

8. Klein, L.A.: Sensor technologies and data requirements for ITS (2001)

9. Anagnostopoulos, C.-N., Anagnostopoulos, I.E., Psoroulas, I.D., Loumos, V., Kayafas, E.: License plate recognition from still images and video sequences: A survey. IEEE Transactions on Intelligent Transportation Systems 9(3), 377–391 (2008)

10. Anagnostopoulos, C.N.E., Anagnostopoulos, I.E., Loumos, V., Kayafas, E.: A license plate-recognition algorithm for intelligent transportation system applications. IEEE Transactions on Intelligent Transportation Systems 7(3), 377–392 (2006)

11. Kemper, A., Neumann, T.: Hyper: A hybrid oltp&olap main memory database system based on virtual memory snapshots. In: 2011 IEEE 27th International Conference on Data Engineering (ICDE), pp. 195–206. IEEE (2011)

12. Lake, P., Crowther, P.: In-memory databases. In: Concise Guide to Databases, pp. 183–197. Springer (2013)

13. Färber, F., May, N., Lehner, W., Große, P., Müller, I., Rauhe, H., Dees, J.: The sap hana database–an architecture overview. IEEE Data Eng. Bull. 35(1), 28–33 (2012)

14. Chang, S.-L., Chen, L.-S., Chung, Y.-C., Chen, S.-W.: Automatic license plate recognition. IEEE Transactions on Intelligent Transportation Systems 5(1), 42–53 (2004)

15. Wen, Y., Lu, Y., Yan, J., Zhou, Z., von Deneen, K.M., Shi, P.: An algorithm for license plate recognition applied to intelligent transportation system. IEEE Transactions on Intelligent Transportation Systems 12(3), 830–845 (2011)

16. Du, S., Ibrahim, M., Shehata, M., Badawy, W.: Automatic license plate recognition (alpr): a state-of-the-art review. IEEE Transactions on Circuits and Systems for Video Technology 23(2), 311–325 (2013)

17. Hongliang, B., Changping, L.: A hybrid license plate extraction method based on edge statistics and morphology. In: Proceedings of the 17th International Conference on Pattern Recognition, ICPR 2004, vol. 2, pp. 831–834. IEEE (2004)

18. Lewis, D.D.: Naive (bayes) at forty: The independence assumption in information retrieval. In: Nédellec, C., Rouveirol, C. (eds.) ECML 1998. LNCS, vol. 1398, pp. 4–15. Springer, Heidelberg (1998)

Author Index

Cao, Jian 11
Chen, Congyang 35
Chen, Jian 49
Chen, Jinjun 35

Dou, Wanchun 93
Duan, Hua 1

Feng, Shanshan 75

Ge, Jidong 21
Ge, Yuhang 21

Hu, Haiyang 21
Hu, Hao 21

Ji, Yu 49
Jia, Guochao 93

Li, Chuanyi 21
Li, Siyun 11
Li, Xiao 75

Liu, Cong 1
Liu, Jianxun 35
Liu, Xiao 59
Liu, Xingmei 49
Liu, Yan 93
Lu, Faming 1
Luo, Bin 21

Ou, Huisi 75

Tao, Xu 93

Wang, Futian 59
Wang, Qiudan 59
Wen, Yiping 35

Yao, Feng 21
Yu, Yang 49

Zeng, Qingtian 1
Zhao, Zhou 59
Zhou, Yu 21

Printed in the United States
By Bookmasters